Child & Adolescent Psychiatry Clinical Cases

Alcides Amador, MD

Child & Adolescent Psychiatry Clinical Cases by Alcides Amador

Contents

Dedication

I dedicate this book to my parents, brother, and grandmother who have supported me through all my endeavors.

Preface

Throughout my journey in medical school, residency, and fellowship, I found that there was lack of clinical cases to help reinforce topics in Child & Adolescent Psychiatry. I have created this book to help address this. My clinical experience and Evidence Based Medicine research aided me in the creation of the cases in the book. The book's conception and completion took over one year, in one of the hardest times in recent history – the COVID-19 Pandemic. I hope the reader finds the cases in this book to be helpful in reinforcing topics in Child & Adolescent Psychiatry.

About the Author

Dr. Alcides Amador is Board Certified in Psychiatry and Child & Adolescent Psychiatry, by The American Board of Psychiatry and Neurology. He is an Assistant Professor of Psychiatry at The University of Texas Rio Grande Valley School of Medicine and is the Psychiatry Clerkship Director as well. He received his medical degree from Baylor College of Medicine and completed his residency and fellowship training in Psychiatry and Child & Adolescent Psychiatry from The University of Texas Medical Branch at Galveston.

Introduction

Child & Adolescent Psychiatry Clinical Cases contains 50 Cases that cover topics such as but not limited to Depressive Disorders, Anxiety Disorders, Psychotic Disorders, and Bipolar Disorders, that can impact Children & Adolescents. DSM-5 criteria were used in the creation of the clinical cases found in this book and care was taken to include references to the medical literature.

The 50 cases contain vignettes followed by multiple choice questions (255 in total). At the end of each case, you can find the answers and references.

Disclaimer

This work is provided "as is". The author of this book has taken care to make certain that the diagnostic criteria and recommended treatment options presented in the book as it relates to the cases found in this book are accurate and are in line with the standard of care at the time of its creation. However, as mental health and medicine are fields that continually evolve and unique situations may require treatment recommendations not contained in this book, it is the duty of the healthcare professional to consult various resources such as but not limited to the product information sheet of medications, most recent diagnostic guidelines, and most recent treatment guidelines when diagnosing and treating patients. Human errors and mechanical/technological errors do sometimes occur, so the author encourages the reader to confirm the information provided in this book with other sources. The author takes no responsibility for decisions made by healthcare professionals as they treat their patients.

This book is no substitute for an individual assessment by a healthcare professional. To the maximum extent as permitted under applicable law, no responsibility is assumed by the author for any injury and/or damage to persons or property, as a matter of products liability, negligence law or otherwise, or from any reference to or use by any person of this work.

Case List

Case 1

A 14 year old girl presents with her mother for an evaluation. She is currently taking Venlafaxine XR 75 mg daily and Aripiprazole 5 mg daily. She started both medications 3 months ago, after not responding to treatment with Fluoxetine and Escitalopram. 6 months ago, she started isolating herself from friends and family, her artwork changed, from positive drawings to negative drawings. She no longer seemed as interested in things and felt tired despite being able to sleep over 11 hours a day. Her mood was irritable, which was different from her usually pleasant mood. Her grades at school decreased since she could not focus on her schoolwork. She attempted suicide before being started on medication. She reports her mood is somewhat improved, but she still does not feel like herself.

Multiple Choice Questions:

1. What is the diagnosis or diagnoses? – Choose all answers that apply

A. Major Depressive Disorder

B. Bipolar 1 Disorder

C. Disruptive Mood Dysregulation Disorder

D. Social Anxiety Disorder

E. None of the Above

2. What metabolic labs should you order to monitor for Aripiprazole's possible metabolic side effects? Choose all answers that apply.

A. UPT

B. Vitamin D

C. HbA1c

D. TSH

E. Lipid Panel

3. Which medication that the patient has tired has the shortest half-life?

A. Aripiprazole

B. Venlafaxine XR

C. Escitalopram

D. Their half-lives are all equal

4. Which medication that the patient is taking is most likely to cause Akathisia?

A. Aripiprazole

B. Venlafaxine XR

C. Escitalopram

D. All are equally likely to cause Akathisia

5. The patient and parent report that in addition to medication, the patient has also been receiving therapy where her therapist has been having her exam her automatic thoughts. Which of the following treatments is she likely receiving?

A. CBT

B. DBT

C. IPT

D. Psychodynamic

E. None of the Above

References & Answers:

1.

Answer: A. Per the history Major Depressive Disorder is the most appropriate answer.

DSM-5. Depressive Disorders. Major Depressive Disorder. Pages 160-168.

2.

Answer: C, E. Antipsychotics are known to have metabolic side effects, the most appropriate answers are to check Lipid Panel and HbA1c.

Aripiprazole FDA Package Insert. 06/2020. https://www.otsuka-us.com/sites/g/files/qhldwo2286/files/media/Abilify-PI.pdf. Date Accessed: 03-13-2021.

Venlafaxine Extended Release Tablets FDA Package Insert. 2012. https://www.accessdata.fda.gov/drugsatfda_docs/label/2012/022104s009lbl.pdf. Date Accessed: 03-13-2021.

Escitalopram FDA Package Insert. 2017. https://www.accessdata.fda.gov/drugsatfda_docs/label/2017/021323s047lbl.pdf. Date Accessed: 03-13-2021.

3.

Answer: B. Out of the listed medications, Venlafaxine XR has the shortest half-life.

Dulcan, M.K. Dulcan's Textbook of Child and Adolescent Psychiatry. 2nd Edition 2016. Antipsychotic Medications. Chapter 38

4.

Answer: A. Out of the listed medications, Aripiprazole is the most likely to cause Akathisia.

Aripiprazole FDA Package Insert. 06/2020. https://www.otsuka-us.com/sites/g/files/qhldwo2286/files/media/Abilify-PI.pdf. Date Accessed: 03-13-2021.

Venlafaxine Extended Release Tablets FDA Package Insert. 2012. https://www.accessdata.fda.gov/drugsatfda_docs/label/2012/022104s009lbl.pdf. Date Accessed: 03-13-2021.

Escitalopram FDA Package Insert. 2017. https://www.accessdata.fda.gov/drugsatfda_docs/label/2017/021323s047lbl.pdf. Date Accessed: 03-13-2021.

5.

Answer: A. Cognitive Behavioral Therapy involves examining cognitive distortions and recognizing automatic thoughts.

Lewis's Child & Adolescent Psychiatry Textbook. 5th Edition. 2018. Chapter 6.2.2. Page 757-787. Page: 762.

Case 2

A 16-year-old male presents for evaluation of mood and concentration.

Parent first noted a problem with the patient's mood in middle school after a falling out with friends. He became sad and no longer seemed like a happy kid, his appetite decreased, he lost weight, he was sleeping too much, his energy was low, and his movements seemed slow. He also lost interest in playing sports which he really enjoyed prior to the falling out with his friends. He started to keep to himself in his room. Parent also found a suicide note and when questioned about it the patient denied writing it. It took about 2-3 months for his sad mood to resolve.

For the past few weeks, the patient's mood has been too elevated, energy levels are too high, self-esteem elevated - he has been saying that he's extremely more intelligent than other kids and has been overly flirtatious with classmates. He has been talking a lot and has been researching artificial intelligence late into the night and pacing around the house. He now seems like the life of the party.

Multiple Choice Questions:

1. What is the diagnosis or diagnoses? – Choose all answers that apply

    A. Major Depressive Disorder
    B. Substance Abuse Disorder
    C. Schizophrenia
    D. Bipolar Disorder
    E. None of the Above

2. Which of the following psychotherapies used for this disorder focuses on keeping routines and a consistent sleep schedule.

    A. Cognitive Behavioral Therapy
    B. Dialectical Behavioral Therapy
    C. Family Focused Therapy
    D. Interpersonal & Social Rhythm Therapy
    E. Multi Family Psychoeducation Group Therapy

3. Which of the following medications would be the best choice in treatment?

    A. Sertraline
    B. Lurasidone
    C. Aripiprazole
    D. Venlafaxine
    E. Risperidone

4. Which of the following disorders is most comorbid with the disorder in this case?

    A. Oppositional Defiant Disorder
    B. Attention Deficit Hyperactivity Disorder
    C. Conduct Disorder
    D. Anxiety Disorder

References & Answers:

1. **Answer: D.** The patient has a history of a major depressive episode and is currently manic. He meets the criteria for Bipolar I Disorder, current episode manic.
DSM-5. Bipolar & Related Disorders – Bipolar I Disorder. Pages: 123-132.

2. **Answer: D.** Interpersonal & Social Rhythm Therapy teaches patients the importance of keeping routines and a consistent sleep schedule.
Lewis's Child & Adolescent Psychiatry – 5th Edition – Chapter 5.4.2 – Page 492 – Psychosocial Treatments.

3.

Answer: C. The risk of weight gain in Risperidone is higher than in Aripiprazole, so Aripiprazole is the first best choice.

Aripiprazole FDA Package Insert. 06/2020. https://www.otsuka-us.com/sites/g/files/qhldwo2286/files/media/Abilify-PI.pdf. Date Accessed: 03-13-2021.

Cooper SJ, Reynolds GP; With expert co-authors (in alphabetical order):, Barnes T, England E, Haddad PM, Heald A, Holt R, Lingford-Hughes A, Osborn D, McGowan O, Patel MX, Paton C, Reid P, Shiers D, Smith J. BAP guidelines on the management of weight gain, metabolic disturbances and cardiovascular risk associated with psychosis and antipsychotic drug treatment. J Psychopharmacol. 2016 Aug;30(8):717-48. **Table 2.**

4.

Answer: B. Attention Deficit Hyperactivity Disorder is the most comorbid disorder in patients with Bipolar Disorder.

Lewis's Child & Adolescent Psychiatry – 5th Edition – Chapter 5.4.2 – Page 486 – Comorbidity.

Case 3

An 8-year-old girl presents for evaluation of excessive talking.

Since age 6 the parent reports that the patient talked too much. The talking was so excessive that children at school and adults would try and avoid talking to the patient. The patient talks about every detail of the things she has done or is doing. For example, if she used 10 napkins instead of using 4 napkins during the day, she will tell everyone about it. Other things the parent has noticed is that if they make an extra stop while going somewhere, the patient will let everyone know that it was not in the original plan and her parent was not honest with the original plans. The patient has also been washing her hands too much. On several occasions she has washed and dried her hands so much that her hands have become dried and have bled from all the hand washing and drying. The patient reports that she feels the need to talk and to be truthful. She does report that her handwashing has caused her to get in trouble at school because of how long it takes her to wash and dry her hands.

Multiple Choice Questions:

1. What is the diagnosis or diagnoses? – Choose all answers that apply

- A. Obsessive Compulsive Disorder
- B. Generalized Anxiety Disorder
- C. Attention Deficit Hyperactivity Disorder
- D. Schizophrenia
- E. Other Specified Schizophrenia Spectrum and Other Psychotic Disorder

2. Which psychotherapy would be most appropriate to treat the patient?

- A. Dialectical Behavioral Therapy
- B. Habit Reversal Training
- C. Exposure and Response Prevention
- D. Psychodynamic Psychotherapy
- E. Interpersonal Psychotherapy Treatment

3. If psychotherapy does not ameliorate the symptoms sufficiently what medication is indicated?

- A. Citalopram
- B. Venlafaxine
- C. Haloperidol
- D. Sertraline
- E. Risperidone

4. Which of the following assessment tools would be most appropriate to use in this case?

    A. PHQ-9
    B. CY-BOCS
    C. SCARED
    D. GAD-7
    E. CDRS-R

References & Answers:

1. **Answer: A**. This patient meets criteria for Obsessive Compulsive Disorder. It is not uncommon for young children to have difficulty with explaining why they do the compulsions. The patient is compelled to tell the truth which has led to excessive talking and compelled to wash her hands.

DSM-5. Obsessive-Compulsive Disorder and Related Disorders. Obsessive-Compulsive Disorder. Pages: 237-242.

2. **Answer: C**. Exposure and Response Prevention would be the most appropriate type of therapy for this patient. Exposure and Response Prevention is a type of Cognitive Behavioral Therapy that is used to treated Obsessive Compulsive Disorder.

Dulcan's Textbook of Child & Adolescent Psychiatry 2nd Edition - Chapter 17 - OCD

3. **Answer: D**. Sertraline is FDA approved for the Treatment of OCD in children ages 6 and older. The Pediatric OCD Treatment Study provides strong evidence for the use of Sertraline and Cognitive Behavioral Therapy in the treatment of pediatric OCD.

Pediatric OCD Treatment Study (POTS) Team. Cognitive-behavior therapy, sertraline, and their combination for children and adolescents with obsessive-compulsive disorder: the Pediatric OCD Treatment Study (POTS) randomized controlled trial. JAMA. 2004 Oct 27;292(16):1969-76.

Sertraline. FDA Package Insert. 12/2017.
https://www.accessdata.fda.gov/drugsatfda_docs/label/2017/019839s091lbl.pdf. Date Accessed: 6-26-2021.

4. **Answer: B**. The most appropriate choice would be the CY-BOCS (Children's Yale-Brown Obsessive Compulsive Scale). It is based off the Yale-Brown Obsessive Compulsive Scale. It can help identify the most prominent OCD symptoms.

Dulcan's Textbook of Child & Adolescent Psychiatry 2nd Edition - Chapter 17 – OCD.

Assessment Scales in Child and Adolescent Psychiatry. 2006. Frank C Verhulst, MD. Jan van der Ende. Children's Yale-Brown Obsessive Compulsive Scale (CY-BOCS). Page 76.

Geller et al. Practice Parameter for the Assessment and Treatment of Children and Adolescents With

Obsessive-Compulsive Disorder. J. Am. Acad. Child Adolesc. Psychiatry, 2012;51(1):98 –113.

Case 4

A 16-year-old male presents for evaluation of trouble sleeping at night.

He reports having trouble sleeping at night. He believes his worries started in 10th grade; he is currently in 11ᵗʰ grade. He reports that during this time he found himself worrying a lot about how he was going to pay for higher education, if he would be successful in the future, would think about past conversations with people and how they could of gone better, worrying about what other people would think about him, worrying about embarrassing himself in front of others, and worried about not being able to calm down and control his worries. He feels like he worries too much. He struggles with the worries all the time even if he is at home, especially at night. These worries cause him to feel tense and makes it hard for him to relax and go to sleep.

Multiple Choice Questions:

1. What is the diagnosis or diagnoses? – Choose all answers that apply

    A. Social Anxiety Disorder
    B. Generalized Anxiety Disorder
    C. Panic Disorder
    D. Agoraphobia
    E. Separation Anxiety Disorder

2. Which psychotherapy would be most appropriate to treat the patient?

    A. Exposure and Response Prevention
    B. Interpersonal Psychotherapy Treatment
    C. Dialectical Behavioral Therapy
    D. Cognitive Behavioral Therapy
    E. Psychodynamic Psychotherapy

3. If psychotherapy does not ameliorate the symptoms sufficiently what medication is indicated?

    A. Citalopram
    B. Duloxetine
    C. Venlafaxine
    D. Escitalopram
    E. Fluoxetine

4. Which of the following assessment tools would be most appropriate to use in this case?

  A. PHQ-9
  B. CY-BOCS
  C. SCARED
  D. CDRS-R
  E. CARS

References & Answers:

1. **Answer: B.** His worries are best explained by Generalized Anxiety Disorder. He worries about several different situations and finds it hard to control the worries. His anxiety has some social anxiety elements but does not meet criteria for Social Anxiety Disorder, since he worries even when at home, where he is not being evaluated by others.

    DSM-5. Anxiety Disorder. Generalized Anxiety Disorder. Page 222 – 226.

2. **Answer: D.** Cognitive Behavioral Therapy has good evidence for the treatment of Generalized Anxiety Disorder. A well-known type of CBT is called Coping Cat.

    Lewis's Child & Adolescent Psychiatry Textbook. 5th Edition. 2018. Chapter 5.5. Page 514.

3. **Answer: B**. Duloxetine is the only FDA approved treatment for Generalized Anxiety Disorder in children ages 7 and older.

    Cymbalta (Duloxetine) FDA Package Insert. 05/2020. https://www.accessdata.fda.gov/drugsatfda_docs/label/2020/021427s053lbl.pdf. Date Accessed: 06-27-2021.

4. **Answer: C.** The SCARED (Screen for Child Anxiety Related Emotional Disorders), screens for several anxiety disorders such as: panic disorder, generalized anxiety disorder, separation anxiety disorder, and social anxiety disorder. There is a self-report version and a parent-report version.

    Lewis's Child & Adolescent Psychiatry Textbook. 5th Edition. 2018. Chapter 5.5. Page 513.
    Assessment Scales in Child and Adolescent Psychiatry. 2006.
    Frank C Verhulst, MD. Jan van der Ende. Screen for Child Anxiety Related Emotional Disorders. Page 62.

Case 5

A 13-year-old girl referred by her pediatrician for problems arising from bullying.

The patient reports that she first noted problems with her mood when she was 12. Prior to this she had no mood problems. Around this time, she started getting bullied at school. The parent reports that she believes the patient started to get bullied because she has Absence Seizures and has also had Generalized Tonic-Clonic Seizures. There have been several episodes of Generalized Tonic-Clonic Seizures that have happened at school. The patient describes her mood as feeling like no one cared about her and was feeling very sad. She used to enjoy playing outside with her siblings, playing games, and singing but she does not find things fun anymore. If allowed to, she could sleep for over 8 hours a day and despite sleeping many hours her energy levels are low. The patient's mother cries when the patient reveals that she has been having thoughts about not wanting to be alive anymore. The parent feels like the patient's mood has been getting worse over the past month.

Additionally, the patient was diagnosed with ADHD by her pediatrician when she was 10. Her current medications are: Methylphenidate ER 27 mg daily, Ethosuximide 500 mg daily, Zonisamide 200 mg daily, and Fluoxetine 10 mg daily.

Multiple Choice Questions:

1. What is the diagnosis or diagnoses? – Choose all answers that apply

A. Bipolar Disorder

B. Major Depressive Disorder

C. Disruptive Mood Dysregulation Disorder

D. Adjustment Disorder with depressed mood

2. Considering the patient's Epilepsy, which medication is contraindicated?

A. Fluoxetine

B. Methylphenidate

C. Sertraline

D. Venlafaxine

E. None of the Above

3. Which medication that she is taking could cause kidney stones?

A. Fluoxetine

B. Zonisamide

C. Ethosuximide

D. Methylphenidate

4. Which of the following disorder occurs more commonly in children with Epilepsy than children without Epilepsy?

A. Schizophrenia

B. Attention Deficit Hyperactivity Disorder

C. Major Depressive Disorder

D. Bipolar Disorder

E. Post-Traumatic Stress Disorder

F. Generalized Anxiety Disorder

5. Children with Absence Seizures have EEG's with which finding?

A. Spike and Wave

B. Triphasic Waves

C. Periodic Lateralized Epileptiform Discharges

D. Generalized Slowing

E. Periodic Sharp Waves

References & Answers:

1. **Answer: B**. The patient meets criteria for Major Depressive Disorder. She has depressed mood, hypersomnia, decreased energy, anhedonia, and thoughts about not wanting to be alive anymore.

   DSM-5. Depressive Disorder. Major Depressive Disorder. Page 160-168.

2. **Answer: E.** None of the listed medications are contraindicated in the treatment for this patient.

   Trivedi MH, Kurian BT. Managing depressive disorders in patients with epilepsy. Psychiatry (Edgmont). 2007;4(1):26-34.

   Kanner AM. The treatment of depressive disorders in epilepsy: what all neurologists should know. Epilepsia. 2013 Mar;54 Suppl 1:3-12.

   Williams AE, Giust JM, Kronenberger WG, Dunn DW. Epilepsy and attention-deficit hyperactivity disorder: links, risks, and challenges. Neuropsychiatr Dis Treat. 2016;12:287-296. Published 2016 Feb 9. doi:10.2147/NDT.S81549

3. **Answer: B**. Kidney Stone formation is a potential complication from taking Zonisamide.

   Zonisamide. FDA Package Insert. April 2020. https://www.accessdata.fda.gov/drugsatfda_docs/label/2020/020789s036lbl.pdf. Date Accessed: 06-27-2021.

4. **Answer: B**. ADHD occurs more commonly in Children with Epilepsy than Children without Epilepsy.

   Epilepsy and ADHD. https://www.epilepsy.com/learn/challenges-epilepsy/moods-and-behavior/mood-and-behavior-101/epilepsy-and-adhd. Date Accessed: 02/01/2021.

   Williams AE, Giust JM, Kronenberger WG, Dunn DW. Epilepsy and attention-deficit hyperactivity disorder: links, risks, and challenges. Neuropsychiatr Dis Treat. 2016;12:287-296. Published 2016 Feb 9. doi:10.2147/NDT.S81549

   Wiggs KK, Chang Z, Quinn PD, Hur K, Gibbons R, Dunn D, Brikell I, Larsson H, D'Onofrio BM. Attention-deficit/hyperactivity disorder medication and seizures. Neurology. 2018 Mar 27;90(13):e1104-e1110.

5. **Answer. A.** Spike and Wave is the EEG finding associated with Absence Seizures.

   St. Louis, EK, Frey, LC (Eds.). Electroencephalography (EEG): An introductory text and atlas of normal and abnormal findings in adults, children and infants. Chicago, IL: American Epilepsy Society; 2016. http://dx.doi.org/10.5698/978-0-9979756-0-4. Page 66.

Case 6

A 6 year old boy brought in by his mother for evaluation of his behavior at home and school. For the past few years, she has felt like he is not developing appropriately. He is very interested in frogs. It has gotten to the point where he will bring several frogs into the home and to school. He also spends many hours a day drawing frogs, using 1 ream of paper every 5 days, and has a tantrum when told to stop. They have started limiting the amount of time he has on his smart tablet, since he will watch the same show for hours and hours and will often repeat catch phrases from the show over and over. He has a very strict bedtime routine and if it is not followed, he will have a tantrum. Overall, he does not do well when routines are changed. He has not been able to make friends at school, he has a hard time engaging in conversations with children and adults, and tends to not look people in the eye. He gets irritated easily. He takes no medications and is described as a healthy child by his pediatrician.

Multiple Choice Questions:

1. What is the diagnosis or diagnoses? – Choose all answers that apply

A. Disruptive Mood Dysregulation Disorder

B. Social Anxiety Disorder

C. Obsessive Compulsive Disorder

D. Autism Spectrum Disorder

E. Social Communication Disorder

F. Developmentally Appropriate Behavior

2. Which of the following testing should you order next?

A. Genetic Testing

B. Urine Analysis

C. MRI - Brain

D. CT - Brain

E. EEG

3. What medication can you consider to treat his irritability?

A. Valproic Acid

B. Trileptal

C. Aripiprazole

D. Quetiapine

E. Sertraline

4. Which therapy option would be beneficial to the patient?

A. Cognitive Behavioral Therapy

B. Psychodynamic Psychotherapy

C. Psychoanalysis

D. Dialectical Behavioral Therapy

E. Applied Behavioral Analysis

5. Children with which of the following genetic disorders has a higher risk of also having the disorder the patient has?

A. Tuberous Sclerosis

B. Tay–Sachs disease

C. Phenylketonuria

D. Sickle Cell Anemia

E. Hepatolenticular Degeneration

References & Answers:

1. Answer: D. The patient meets criteria for Autism Spectrum Disorder.

DSM-5. Neurodevelopmental Disorders. Autism Spectrum Disorder. Page 50-59.

2. **Answer: A.** AACAP recommends that all children & adolescents diagnosed with Autism Spectrum Disorder, undergo Genetic Testing. In the absence of an abnormal physical exam the other suggested lab work is not warranted at this time.

   Volkmar et al. Practice Parameter for the Assessment and Treatment of Children and Adolescents With Autism Spectrum Disorder. J. Am. Acad. Child Adolesc. Psychiatry, 2014;53(2):237–257

3. Answer: C. Out of the list medications only Aripiprazole is FDA approved to treat irritability associated with Autism Spectrum Disorder in children ages 6 and older.

Aripiprazole FDA Package Insert. February 2020. https://www.accessdata.fda.gov/drugsatfda_docs/label/2020/021436s044s045,021713s035s036,021729s027s028,021866s029s030lbl.pdf. Date Accessed: 06-28-2021.

4. Answer: E. The therapy option for the patient that is most appropriate at this time is Applied Behavioral Analysis. It uses operant conditioning as a core component. This therapy helps decrease maladaptive behaviors and increases appropriate behaviors, by analyzing the antecedents and consequences of behaviors.

Lewis's Child & Adolescent Psychiatry Textbook. 5th Edition. 2018. Chapter 6.2.6. Page 766. Chapter 6.2.4. Pages: 796-797

5. Answer: A. Out of the listed disorders, Tuberous Sclerosis has the highest risk of also having Autism Spectrum Disorder. It is estimated that approximately 50% of patients with Tuberous Sclerosis Complex are also diagnosed with Autism Spectrum Disorder.

Julich K., Sahin M. (2014) Autism Spectrum Disorders in Tuberous Sclerosis. In: Patel V., Preedy V., Martin C.(eds) Comprehensive Guide to Autism. Springer, New York, NY. https://doi.org/10.1007/978-1-4614-4788-7_184

Jeste SS, Varcin KJ, Hellemann GS, et al. Symptom profiles of autism spectrum disorder in tuberous sclerosis complex. Neurology. 2016;87(8):766-772. doi:10.1212/WNL.0000000000003002

Case 7

A 16 year old who presents for evaluation of problems making friends. The patient reports that he has a hard time knowing what to talk about with other people and this has made it hard for him to make friends. He reports that there was a person he liked at his high school and that he thought by talking to them they would then start dating, which would lead to him having friends at school. He tried to talk to this person, but the conversation did not go well. His parents report that ever since he was little, his social skills have been awkward, it's hard for him to have smooth back and forth conversations, and has a hard time picking up on social cues & body language. He likes to spend most of his time watching baseball when not at school, he is extremely knowledgeable about obscure baseball facts. They have a hard time doing spontaneous activities as a family, since he does not like changes to family routines. If a spontaneous activity happens, he will become very irritable. They are hoping that there is a way to teach him how to make friends. The patient reports to feeling a bit down since he has not been able to make friends. He gets all A's in school and is in the most advanced classes.

Multiple Choice Questions:

1. What is the diagnosis or diagnoses? – Choose all answers that apply

A. Disruptive Mood Dysregulation Disorder

B. Social Anxiety Disorder

C. Obsessive Compulsive Disorder

D. Autism Spectrum Disorder

E. Social Communication Disorder

F. Developmentally Appropriate Behavior

2. Which of the following therapies would most likely be helpful for him?

A. Psychoanalytic Therapy

B. Interpersonal Psychotherapy

C. Cognitive Behavioral Therapy

D. Social Skills Group Therapy

E. Applied Behavioral Analysis

3. It is estimated that 50% of children with a certain genetic mutation can meet criteria for the disorder the patient has. Which of the following is the gene this has been linked to?

A. FMR-1

B. PMP22

C. SCA1

D. ATM

E. ApoE4

4. Which of the following screening scales would have been helpful to identify the patient's disorder when he was a toddler?

A. SCARED

B. PHQ-9

C. YMRS

D. MCHAT

E. DISC

5. Which of the following findings is thought to be a good prognostic factor for the condition the patient has?

A. Epilepsy

B. Functional language by age 5

C. Intellectual Disability

D. None of the above

References & Answers:

1. Answer: D. The patient meets criteria for Autism Spectrum Disorder. It is likely that the patient is on the higher end of the spectrum and now that he is older the symptoms are more readily apparent.

DSM-5. Neurodevelopmental Disorders. Autism Spectrum Disorder. Pages 50-59.

2. Answer: D. At this time Social Skills Group Therapy would be the most helpful therapy for this patient. A naturalistic social skills group were patients are higher-functioning would be the ideal group for him. For patients that are lower functioning a curriculum based social skills group would be more appropriate.

Lewis's Child & Adolescent Psychiatry Textbook. 5th Edition. 2018. Chapter 6.2.6. Pages 830-832

3. Answer: A. FMR-1 mutations can lead to Fragile X Syndrome, which is one of the Genetic Syndromes that increases patients risk of having Autism Spectrum Disorder.

Lewis's Child & Adolescent Psychiatry Textbook. 5th Edition. 2018. Chapter 3.3.3. Pages 265, 267-269.

4. Answer: D. The M-CHAT (Modified Checklist for Autism in Toddlers) is the most appropriate choice. It is indicated for use in toddlers up to age 30 months. The M-CHAT is filled out by the parent.

Assessment Scales in Child and Adolescent Psychiatry. 2006. Frank C Verhulst, MD. Jan van der Ende. Pages 141-142.

5. Answer: B. Functional language by age 5 is a good prognostic factor for Autism Spectrum Disorder.

DSM-5. Neurodevelopmental Disorders. Autism Spectrum Disorder. Pages 56-57.

Case 8

A 16 year old girl who presents with her parent with concerns about how she is dealing with stressors at home.

The parent reports that their spouse has been having an affair and this has led to many arguments at home. It has reached a point where the patient tries to calm both parents down whenever they argue. The parents now try not to argue in front of the patient. The parent is concerned because when she asks the patient if she wants to talk about the situation, the patient has told her that she does not want to talk about it. The parent is concerned if the patient does not talk about it that she will develop emotional problems later in life.

The patient reports that she does feel sad and stressed that her parents are having problems in their marriage. However, she still enjoys things, considers herself a happy person, and energy levels are good. She likes hanging out with her friends, playing sports, and being around her parents. She is getting good grades at school and considers herself to be a responsible person. She reports that there was one time she felt like she did not want to be alive anymore, this happened in the context of when the whole family found out about the affair. However, she reports that this was only a momentary thought and she had no intent or plan. She reports that this happened 3 months ago and has never come up again. She reports that she would never kill herself because that would not solve anything, is against her religious beliefs, and she does not want to cut her life short.

Multiple Choice Questions:

1. What is the diagnosis or diagnoses? – Choose all answers that apply

A. Major Depressive Disorder

B. Adjustment Disorder

C. Borderline Personality Disorder

D. Separation Anxiety Disorder

E. None of the Above

2. What is the ratio of mood disorders in adolescents: Male to Female

A. 1:1

B. 1: 2

C. 1:3

D. 1:4

E. 1:5

3. What are the estimated suicide completion rates in youth: Male to Female

A. 1:1

B. 2: 1

C. 3:1

D. 4:1

E. 5:1

4. What is the approximate percentage of youth with suicidal ideation that go on to make a suicidal plan?

A. 25%

B. 33%

C. 50%

D. 66%

E. 75%

F. 100%

5. Which of the following scales would be best to assess immediate risk of suicide in an acute care setting?

A. PHQ-9

B. SCARED

C. C-SSRS

D. GAD-7

E. K-SADS

F. DISC

References & Answers:

1. **Answer E.** There is no psychiatric disorder in this patient with the available history. It is reasonable for some to feel sad and stressed in these types of situations. You can label this as: Child Affected by Parental Relationship Distress. V61.29 (Z62.989).

   DSM-5. Other Conditions That Maybe A Focus of Clinical Attention. Problems Related to Family Upbringing. Page 715-716.

2. **Answer C.** The ratio of mood disorders in adolescents – Male: Female – is 1:3.

   Lewis's Child & Adolescent Psychiatry Textbook. 5th Edition. 2018. Chapter 5.4.1. Page 473.

3. **Answer E.** The estimated suicide completion rates in youth – Male : Female is 5:1,

   Dulcan's Textbook of Child and Adolescent Psychiatry. 2nd Edition 2016. Chapter 27.

4. **Answer B.** Approximately 33% of youth with suicidal ideation go on to make a suicidal plan

   Dulcan's Textbook of Child and Adolescent Psychiatry. 2nd Edition 2016. Chapter 27.

5. **Answer C.** The C-SSRs (The Columbia-Suicide Severity Rating Scale), would be the best choice to use to assess for immediate risk of suicide in an acute care setting.

   Assessment Scales in Child and Adolescent Psychiatry. 2006. Frank C Verhulst, MD. Jan van der Ende.

   Lewis's Child & Adolescent Psychiatry Textbook. 5th Edition. 2018. Chapter 4.6. Page 345-346

   Dulcan's Textbook of Child and Adolescent Psychiatry. 2nd Edition 2016. Chapter 27.

   Zuckerbrot RA, Cheung A, Jensen PS, et al. Guidelines for Adolescent Depression in Primary Care (GLAD-PC): Part I. Practice Preparation, Identification, Assessment, and Initial Management. Pediatrics. 2018;141(3):e20174081.

   https://www.aap.org/en-us/professional-resources/qualityimprovement/ProjectRedDE/Pages/Depression.aspx. Adolescent Depression Screening. American Academy of Pediatrics. Accessed: 02-08-2021.

   Walter, H. et al. Clinical Practice Guideline for the Assessment and Treatment of Children and Adolescents With Anxiety Disorders. J Am Acad Child Adolesc Psychiatry 2020;59(10):1107–1124.

Case 9

A 12 year old male brought in for evaluation of his mood.

The patient's parent reports that the patient was diagnosed with Intellectual Disability when he was 6 years old. He receives special education services at his school and splits his time in school between special education classes and non-special education classes. For several years she has been very concerned about his mood and is hoping to find out treatment options for his mood. She reports that he gets irritated easily when routines are not followed. In the past he used to scream and throw things when routines were not followed or if they changed. Now his irritability has decreased but it still has been problematic at home and school. She recalls that ever since he was little he would talk nonstop about dinosaurs and if you tried to change the conversation he would get very upset. He still likes to talk about dinosaurs, and he is willing to change the subject for a while before going back to talking about dinosaurs. His social interactions are awkward, and he has a hard time making friends and gets frustrated easily in social situations. The patient reports that it is hard to know how to talk to others and wishes he could make friends. He reports that he gets upset easily when his parents remind him to look at people when he tries to talk with them.

Multiple Choice Questions:

1. What is the diagnosis or diagnoses? – Choose all answers that apply

A. Major Depressive Disorder

B. Bipolar Disorder

C. Disruptive Mood Dysregulation Disorder

D. Autism Spectrum Disorder

E. Schizoaffective Disorder

F. Social Anxiety Disorder

2. In patient's with this disorder what percentage are thought to have intelligence quotients within the normal range?

A. 0%

B. 5%

C. 10%

D. 15%

E. 20%

F. None of the above

3. EEG Abnormalities and Seizure Disorders are thought to occur at what percentage range for these patient's?

A. 10% - 20%

B. 20% - 25%

C. 30% - 35%

D. 40% - 45%

E. 50% - 55%

4. What is the estimated prevalence of this disorder in the USA?

A. 0.5%

B. 1.13%

C. 2.0%

D. 2.4%

E. 3.0%

5. Prenatal Exposure to which of the following has been linked to higher risk to develop the disorder the patient has?

A. Carbamazepine

B. Oxcarbazepine

C. Lamotrigine

D. Valproic Acid

E. None of the above

References & Answers:

1. **Answer D**. The patient meets the criteria for Autism Spectrum Disorder based on the history provided.

DSM-5. Neurodevelopmental Disorders. Autism Spectrum Disorder. Page 50-59.

2. **Answer E.** It is estimated that approximately 20% of patient's with Autism Spectrum Disorder have IQs within the normal range.

Volkmar et al. Practice Parameter for the Assessment and Treatment of Children and Adolescents With Autism Spectrum Disorder2014. J. Am. Acad. Child Adolesc. Psychiatry, 2014;53(2): 241.

3. **Answer B.** 20-25% of patients with Autism Spectrum Disorder are thought to EEG Abnormalities and Seizure Disorders.

Volkmar et al. Practice Parameter for the Assessment and Treatment of Children and Adolescents With Autism Spectrum Disorder2014. J. Am. Acad. Child Adolesc. Psychiatry, 2014;53(2):237–257

4. **Answer B.** The estimated prevalence of Autism Spectrum Disorder in the USA is 1.13%

Volkmar et al. Practice Parameter for the Assessment and Treatment of Children and Adolescents With Autism Spectrum Disorder2014. J. Am. Acad. Child Adolesc. Psychiatry, 2014;53(2):237–257

5. **Answer D.** Prenatal exposure to Valproic Acid increases the risk of a child developing Autism Spectrum Disorder. It is very important to let women know about this increased risk.

Christensen, J. et al. Prenatal Valproate Exposure and Risk of Autism Spectrum Disorders and Childhood Autism JAMA, April 24, 2013—Vol 309, No. 16. Page 1696-1703

Case 10

A 14 year old girl with Autism Spectrum Disorder and Attention Deficit Hyperactivity Disorder presents for follow up. She is on Carbamazepine 200 mg BID, Risperidone 1 mg BID, Clonidine 0.1 mg qhs, and Fluoxetine 20 mg daily. She had labs drawn about a year ago but her parent forgot to bring in the labs for you to review. She has noticed that the patient has been looking sick and has complained of a sore throat, she usually does not get sick and had a fever last night. Besides that, she reports that the patient has been doing fine, she has not gained weight on the medication regimen, and is happy with the current medication regimen.

Multiple Choice Questions:

1. Which of the following labs would be the most indicated in this case?

A. TSH

B. UPT

C. Lipid Panel

D. CBC

E. HbA1c

2. Which medication would be the likely cause of an abnormal CBC in this patient?

A. Clonidine

B. Fluoxetine

C. Risperidone

D. Carbamazepine

3. Which of the following alleles has been associated with an increased risk of Steven Johnson Syndrome?

A. HLA-C*06:02

B. HLA-DR2

C. HLA-DQ2

D. HLA-B*1502

E. HLA–DQB1*06:02

F. None of the above

4. Which of the following medications that the patient is taking has the best evidence for use in irritability in children with Autism Spectrum Disorder?

A. Clonidine

B. Fluoxetine

C. Risperidone

D. Carbamazepine

5. Which monitoring protocol is recommended for Lipid & HbA1c in Child & Adolescent Psychiatry patients on Antipsychotics?

A. Baseline, 1 month, then every 6 months

B. Baseline, 2 months, then every 6 months

C. Baseline, 3 months, then every 6 months

D. Baseline, 4 months, then every 6 months

References & Answers:

1. **Answer D.** The most useful lab at this time would be the CBC. Carbamazepine can cause hematologic abnormalities and could make you more susceptible to get sick.

Lewis's Child & Adolescent Psychiatry Textbook. 5th Edition. 2018. Chapter 5.4.2. Page 494-495, 745-746.

2. **Answer D.** Carbamazepine can cause hematologic abnormalities and could make you more susceptible to get sick, getting a CBC would help you see if there are any hematologic abnormalities present.

Lewis's Child & Adolescent Psychiatry Textbook. 5th Edition. 2018. Chapter 5.4.2. Page 494-495, 745-746.

3. **Answer D.** HLA-B*1502, is the allele that has been associated with an increased risk of Steven Johnson Syndrome. Carbamazepine is one of the medications that is associated with a risk of developing Steven Johnson Syndrome.

Carbamazepine. FDA Package Insert. 03/2018. https://www.accessdata.fda.gov/drugsatfda_docs/label/2018/016608s115_018281_s058_018927s055_020234_s047.pdf. Date Accessed: 07-11-2021.

Delves, P. J. Human Leukocyte Antigen (HLA) System. Merck Manual. https://www.merckmanuals.com/professional/immunology-allergic-disorders/biology-of-the-immune-system/human-leukocyte-antigen-hla-system#. Date Accessed: 02-12-2021.

4. **Answer C.** Risperidone is one of the medications that is FDA approved for the treatment of irritability in children with Autism Spectrum Disorder. The other medication that is approved for this is Aripiprazole.

Risperidone. FDA Package Insert. 02/2021. https://www.accessdata.fda.gov/drugsatfda_docs/label/2021/020272Orig1s083,020588Orig1s071,021444Orig1s057,021346Orig1s061lbl.pdf. Date Accessed: 07-11-202.

Volkmar et al. Practice Parameter for the Assessment and Treatment of Children and Adolescents with Autism Spectrum Disorder. J. Am. Acad. Child Adolesc. Psychiatry, 2014;53(2): 251.

5. **Answer C.** The recommend Lipid & HbA1c monitoring protocol is: Baseline, 3 months, then every 6 months.

Dulcan, M.K. Dulcan's Textbook of Child and Adolescent Psychiatry. 2nd Edition 2016. Chapter 38. Table 38-7, Table 38-8.

Case 11

A 13 year old female brought in by her parents for problems with her behavior. The parents report that she was diagnosed with Autism Spectrum Disorder when she was age 7. She has attended Applied Behavioral Analysis therapy for several years and it has been helpful. However, for over a year now they have noticed that she takes a very long time in the shower, most times for over 60 minutes. When asked by her parents why she takes such a long time, she has told them that she might develop a skin infection if she does not shower right. It has reached a point where she has been late to school every day now. As a result, she has unexcused absences in several classes and is failing those classes. The patient reports that she needs to shower just right and that she needs to do it without making any mistakes. If she makes a mistake while showering, she will need to start over again. The thought of getting a skin infection from not showering just right bothers her daily.

Multiple Choice Questions:

1. What is the diagnosis or diagnoses? – Choose all answers that apply

A. Specific Phobia

B. Generalized Anxiety Disorder

C. Delusional Disorder

D. Brief Psychotic Disorder

E. None of the Above

2. Patient's with the disorder this patient has would benefit from which of the following treatments?

A. Exposure and Response Prevention

B. Psychodynamic Psychotherapy

C. Dialectical Behavioral Therapy

D. Habit Reversal Training

E. Interpersonal and Social Rhythm Therapy

3. Which of the following medications would be the most appropriate for this case?

A. Risperidone

B. Haloperidol

C. Oxcarbazepine

D. Lithium

E. Citalopram

F. None of the above

4. Which of the following disorders has higher rates of comorbidity with the patient's newly discovered diagnosis?

A. Schizophrenia

B. Bipolar Disorder

C. Tourette's Disorder

D. Social Anxiety Disorder

E. Disruptive Mood Dysregulation Disorder

F. None of the above

5. What is the recommend length of treatment with medication at the maximum or tolerated dosage, before considering making a change to the medication in patients with this disorder?

A. 4 Weeks

B. 6 Weeks

C. 8 weeks

D. 10 weeks

E. None of the above

6. Which of the following brain regions is thought to play a role in patient's with the newly diagnosed disorder this patient has?

A. Medulla

B. Hippocampus

C. Pontine Paramedian Reticular Formation

D. Basal Ganglia

E. Superior Colliculus

F. None of the above

References & Answers:

1. Answer E. This patient meets the criteria for Obsessive-Compulsive Disorder she has obsessive thoughts about getting a skin infection and tries to prevent the skin infection by showering just right which usually takes her over 60 minutes.

DSM-5. Obsessive-Compulsive and Related Disorders. Obsessive Compulsive Disorder. Pages 235-242.

2. Answer A. Exposure and Response Prevention is the most appropriate therapy for her OCD. Exposure and Response Prevention is a form of Cognitive Behavioral Therapy that exposes the patient to the feared stimulus and helps them learn how to resist acting on their compulsion.

Dulcan, M.K. Dulcan's Textbook of Child and Adolescent Psychiatry. 2nd Edition 2016. Chapter 17.

Practice Parameter for the Assessment and Treatment of Children and Adolescents with Obsessive-Compulsive Disorder. J. Am. Acad. Child Adolesc. Psychiatry, 2012;51(1): 104 – 106

Exposure and Response Prevention. International OCD Foundation. https://iocdf.org/about-ocd/ocd-treatment/erp/. Date Accessed: 02-13-2021.

3. Answer F. None of the listed medications would be appropriate for the treatment of OCD in this patient. The FDA approved medications for OCD in her age group are Fluoxetine, Fluvoxamine, Sertraline, and Clomipramine.

Practice Parameter for the Assessment and Treatment of Children and Adolescents with Obsessive-Compulsive Disorder. J. Am. Acad. Child Adolesc. Psychiatry, 2012;51(1): 106-108.

Dulcan, M.K. Dulcan's Textbook of Child and Adolescent Psychiatry. 2nd Edition 2016. Chapter 17.

4. Answer C. Out of the listed disorders, Tourette's Disorder has the higher rate of comorbidity with OCD.

Lewis's Child & Adolescent Psychiatry Textbook. 5th Edition. 2018. Chapter 5.6. Page 537-538.

5. Answer D. 10 weeks is the recommended treatment length at the maximum or tolerated dosage before considering a treatment change in medication for the treatment of OCD.

Dulcan, M.K. Dulcan's Textbook of Child and Adolescent Psychiatry. 2nd Edition 2016. Chapter 17.

6. **Answer D.** The Basal Ganglia is thought to play a role in OCD.

Dulcan, M.K. Dulcan's Textbook of Child and Adolescent Psychiatry. 2nd Edition 2016. Chapter 17.

Case 12

A 14-year-old girl who presents with her parent with concerns about stress. The patient reports that several months ago she had an episode of feeling her heart racing fast, feeling shaky, became short of breath, feeling dizzy, sweating, feeling weak, and feeling like she was going to die. This happened during a school trip to a museum while she was talking to her classmates. She felt really embarrassed afterwards. After the school trip, she started having several episodes like these a few times a week that occur without warning. One episode was so severe that she had to go to the Emergency Room. At the Emergency Room her work up was fine and she was told that it was likely that her symptoms were caused by stress. The patient reports that she is very concerned about having more episodes and is no longer hanging out with friends as much because she does not want them to see her get stressed out.

Multiple Choice Questions:

1. What is the diagnosis or diagnoses? – Choose all answers that apply

A. Agoraphobia

B. Generalized Anxiety Disorder

C. Adjustment Disorder

D. Panic Disorder

E. Social Anxiety Disorder

2. Which of the following psychotherapy treatment options is most indicated?

A. Cognitive Behavioral Therapy

B. Dialectical Behavioral Therapy

C. Psychoanalysis

D. Habit Reversal Training

E. None of the Above

3. What is the estimated male to female ratio of this disorder?

A. 1:1

B. 1:2

C. 1:3

D. 1:4

E. 1:5

4. Which of the following would be the most appropriate scale to use in this case

A. PHQ-9

B. CDRS

C. CY-BOCS

D. SCARED

E. CARS

5. Which class of medication has the most evidence in treatment of this disorder in children and adolescents?

A. Antipsychotics

B. Mood Stabilizers

C. SSRIs

D. SNRIs

E. MAOIs

F. TCAs

G. None of the above

6. What is the estimated prevalence of this disorder before the age of 14?

A. <0.1%

B. <0.2%

C.<0.3%

D.<0.4%

E. <0.5%

7. What is the estimated median age of onset for this disorder?

A. 10-14

B. 14-18

C. 20-24

D. 24-28

E. None of the above

8. Which of the following tests would be most appropriate to work up this disorder in this case?

A. MRI

B. CT

C. Bone Survey

D. EKG

E. EMG

References & Answers:

1. Answer D. This patient meets criteria Panic Disorder.

DSM-5. Anxiety Disorders. Panic Disorder. Pages 208-214.

2. Answer A. The most indicated psychotherapy treatment for anxiety in Children & Adolescents is Cognitive Behavioral Therapy.

Lewis's Child & Adolescent Psychiatry Textbook. 5th Edition. 2018. Chapter 5.5.1. Page 514.

Freidl et al. Assessment and Treatment of Anxiety Among Children and Adolescents. Focus (Am Psychiatr Publ). Spring 2017; 15(2): 144–156.

3. Answer B. The estimated male to female ration is 1:2.

DSM-5. Anxiety Disorders. Panic Disorder. Pages 208-214.

4. Answer D. The SCARED would be the most appropriate choice to also screen for other anxiety disorders the patient might have.

Assessment Scales in Child and Adolescent Psychiatry. 2006. Frank C Verhulst, MD. Jan van der Ende. Screen for Child Anxiety Related Emotional Disorders. Page 62.

Lewis's Child & Adolescent Psychiatry Textbook. 5th Edition. 2018. Chapter 5.5.1. Page 513.

5. Answer C. Although there is no FDA approved treatment for Panic Disorder in Children & Adolescents, SSRIs have the most evidence and are the most studied for this disorder in Children & Adolescents.

Freidl et al. Assessment and Treatment of Anxiety Among Children and Adolescents. Focus (Am Psychiatr Publ). Spring 2017; 15(2): 144–156.

Lewis's Child & Adolescent Psychiatry Textbook. 5th Edition. 2018. Chapter 5.5.1. Page 515.

6. Answer D. Panic Disorder is not a common disorder seen in young children. More common to see its development in young adulthood.

DSM-5. Anxiety Disorders. Panic Disorder. Pages 210.

7. Answer C. The median age of onset of Panic Disorder is between the ages of 20-24.

DSM-5. Anxiety Disorders. Panic Disorder. Pages 210.

8. Answer D. Out of the listed choices getting an EKG would be the most appropriate choice, to rule out if cardiac arrhythmias could also be the cause of the patient's symptoms.

Lewis's Child & Adolescent Psychiatry Textbook. 5th Edition. 2018. Chapter 5.5.1. Page 511.

Case 13

A 12 year old male brought in by his parent to talk about stress in the family. A few months ago the parent reports that the patient's father voiced thoughts of not wanting to live anymore and thoughts about wanting to commit suicide if his wife continued to refuse to move the family to a different state. The father wants to move to a different state because his parents died 6 months ago from old age, they lived with the family, and he feels overwhelmed by reminders of his parents. The mother does not think this is a good idea since before the current situation the whole family loved the town. This has led to many loud arguments between both the parents. The arguments have been stressing the patient out, and whenever the parents argue he tries to stop them and sometimes cries. The patient has a lot of friends in town, is a good student, and likes living in the town. The parent is worried that her son will become depressed if the problems at home continue. The patient reports that overall he is a happy kid but he has been feeling stressed out ever since his parents started arguing about moving. He does not like it that his parents have been arguing and he hopes that they do not move. When his parents argue he feels more stressed out and usually screams at them to stop. When his parents do not argue, everything at home goes well and he does not feel stressed. This past weekend he went a friend's house for a sleep over because he got straight A's on his report card. He had fun at the sleep over.

Multiple Choice Questions:

1. What is the diagnosis or diagnoses? – Choose all answers that apply

A. Major Depressive Disorder

B. Disruptive Mood Dysregulation Disorder

C. Post Traumatic Stress Disorder

D. Bipolar Disorder

E. Adjustment Disorder

F. None of the above

2. A few months have passed, and the patient has started to have behavioral problems at school for the past month. He has been yelling at teachers and friends and breaking things at home when he gets upset, he has never done these things before. His parents continue to have arguments at home about moving out of state. He reports being angry about the possibility of moving. What is the diagnosis now?

A. Major Depressive Disorder

B. Disruptive Mood Dysregulation Disorder

C. Intermittent Explosive Disorder

D. Bipolar Disorder

E. Adjustment Disorder

F. None of the above

3. Considering the answer from question 2, at what percentage of frequency is this disorder often diagnosed in a psychiatric consult setting in hospitals?

A. 10%

B. 25%

C. 50%

D. 75%

E. None of the above

4. Considering the answer from question 2, this disorder is most diagnosed in which of the following groups – Chose all answers that apply?

A. Retail Workers

B. Children

C. Teachers

D. Podiatrists

E. Social Workers

F. Military

G. None of the above

5. Considering the answer from question 2, treatment with which of the following is most indicated in this disorder?

A. SSRIs

B. SNRIs

C. Mood Stabilizers

D. Antipsychotics

E. Psychotherapy

F. None of the Above

References & Answers:

1. Answer F. Currently the patient does not meet criteria for a Psychiatric Disorder, his reaction to his parents arguing is not out of the ordinary and can be conceptualized as a Normative Stress Reaction or Child Affected by Parental Relationship Distress.

DSM-5. Trauma and Stressors Related Disorders. Adjustment Disorder. Pages 289.

DSM-5. Other Conditions That May Be a Focus of Clinical Attention. Page 716.

2. Answer E. His current condition is best described as Adjustment Disorder with disturbance of conduct. His distress and reaction to the stress now are more problematic.

DSM-5. Trauma and Stressors Related Disorders. Adjustment Disorder. Pages 286-289.

3. Answer C. The percentage frequency of this disorder is estimated to be about 50% in a psychiatric consult setting in hospitals.

DSM-5. Trauma and Stressors Related Disorders. Adjustment Disorder. Pages 287

4. Answer B & F. The disorder is most diagnosed in the following groups: children and military.

Strain, J. The Adjustment Disorder Diagnosis, Its Importance to Liaison Psychiatry, and its Psychobiology. Int. J. Environ. Res. Public Health 2019, 16, 4645.

5. Answer E. The most indicated treatment for this disorder is Psychotherapy. There is no medication that is FDA approved for treatment of Adjustment Disorder.

Casey, P. et al. Adjustment Disorders: Diagnostic and Treatment Issues. Psychiatric Times. https://www.psychiatrictimes.com/view/adjustment-disorders-diagnostic-and-treatment-issues. Date Accessed: 02-15-2021

Case 14

A 16 year old year old male accompanied by his parents, he needs a new doctor since they just moved to the area a month ago.

The patient reports that he has been feeling sad and anxious for over 3 months. He was not eaten well and has lost about 15 lbs. He has a difficult time falling asleep and staying asleep. He feels like his energy levels are low, and he has started taking naps in his school. A few months ago, he reported to his pastor that he was having thoughts about wanting to die. His parents report that he does not seem to enjoy things anymore and has been having anxiety episodes. They describe his anxiety episodes as him reporting chest discomfort, feeling light-headed, he starts to sweat, he reports feeling hot, and he starts to shake. He actively tries to avoid things that he says could cause him to have more panic attacks. He usually has several panic attacks during the week and they often happen without anything stressful going on.

His pediatrician started him on Desvenlafaxine and Hydroxyzine, about 1 month ago. He reports that his mood and anxiety symptoms have minimally improved. His father takes Desvenlafaxine for his mood problems and has benefited from it, so that is why the patient's pediatrician started him on Desvenlafaxine.

Multiple Choice Questions:

1. What is the diagnosis or diagnoses? – Choose all answers that apply

A. Generalized Anxiety Disorder

B. Major Depressive Disorder with panic attacks

C. Agoraphobia

D. Major Depressive Disorder

E. Social Anxiety Disorder

F. Adjustment Disorder

G. Panic Disorder

2. Which of the following treatments would the patient most likely benefit from?

A. Cognitive Behavioral Therapy

B. Dialectical Behavioral Therapy

C. Interpersonal and Social Rhythm Therapy

D. Psychoanalysis

E. None of the above

3. Which one of the classes of medications would be the best choice for the patient based on the available scientific evidence?

A. SNRIs

B. Beta Blockers

C. Mood Stabilizers

D. Antipsychotics

E. SSRIs

F. None of the above

4. Cognitive Behavioral Therapy and what medication were found to be helpful in the treatment of anxiety in the Child/Adolescent Multimodal Study?

A. Citalopram

B. Sertraline

C. Venlafaxine

D. Duloxetine

E. Fluoxetine

F. Desvenlafaxine

F. None of the above

5. Cognitive Behavioral Therapy and what medication were found to be helpful in treatment of depression in the Treatment for Adolescents with Depression Study.

A. Citalopram

B. Sertraline

C. Venlafaxine

D. Duloxetine

E. Fluoxetine

F. Desvenlafaxine

F. None of the above

6. Which of the following disorders in Children & Adolescents is Desvenlafaxine approved for?

A. Generalized Anxiety Disorder

B. Major Depressive Disorder with panic attacks

C. Agoraphobia

D. Major Depressive Disorder

E. Social Anxiety Disorder

F. Adjustment Disorder

G. Panic Disorder

H. None of the above

7. Desvenlafaxine is what class of medication?

A. SNRIs

B. Beta Blockers

C. Mood Stabilizers

D. Antipsychotics

E. SSRIs

F. None of the above

8. Desvenlafaxine increases the levels of which neurotransmitter?

A. Glutamate

B. Epinephrine

C. Histamine

D. Glycine

E. GABA

F. None of the above

9. Which of the following areas of the brain involved is associated with the neurotransmitters Desvenlafaxine effects?

A. Substantia Nigra

B. Nucleus Accumbens

C. Red Nucleus

D. Subthalamic Nucleus

E. Locus coeruleus

F. None of the above

References & Answers:

1. **Answer D & G.** The patient meets the criteria for Major Depressive Disorder & Panic Disorder.

DSM-5. Depressive Disorders. Major Depressive Disorder. Pages 160-168.

DSM-5. Anxiety Disorders. Panic Disorder. Pages 208-214.

2. **Answer A.** The best treatment out of the options available would be Cognitive Behavioral Therapy.

Freidl, E. et al. Assessment and Treatment of Anxiety Among Children and Adolescents. Focus (Am Psychiatr Publ). Spring 2017; 15(2): 144–156.

Lewis's Child & Adolescent Psychiatry Textbook. 5th Edition. 2018. Chapter 5.4.1. Page 476-477.

3. **Answer E.** SSRIs would be the best medication treatment choice for this patient based on the available evidence.

Lewis's Child & Adolescent Psychiatry Textbook. 5th Edition. 2018. Chapter 5.4.1. Page 476-477.

Lewis's Child & Adolescent Psychiatry Textbook. 5th Edition. 2018. Chapter 5.5.1. Page 515.

4. **Answer B.** Sertraline was the medication used in the Child/Adolescent Multimodal Study and the medication found to be helpful.

Walkup, J. et al. Cognitive Behavioral Therapy, Sertraline, or a Combination in Childhood Anxiety. N Engl J Med 2008;359:2753-66.

5. **Answer E.** Fluoxetine was the medication used in the Treatment for Adolescents with Depression Study.

March, J. et al. The Treatment for Adolescents With Depression Study (TADS). Arch Gen Psychiatry. 2007;64(10):1132-1144

6. **Answer H.** Desvenlafaxine, brand name Pristiq, is not FDA approved for use in children or adolescents.

Pristiq (Desvenlafaxine). FDA Package Insert. 02-2018. https://www.accessdata.fda.gov/drugsatfda_docs/label/2018/021992s042lbl.pdf. Date Accessed: 7-22-2021.

7. **Answer A.** Desvenlafaxine, is a SNRI (Serotonin-Norepinephrine Reuptake Inhibitor).

Pristiq (Desvenlafaxine). FDA Package Insert. 02-2018. https://www.accessdata.fda.gov/drugsatfda_docs/label/2018/021992s042lbl.pdf. Date Accessed: 7-22-2021.

8. **Answer F.** Desvenlafaxine, increases the level of Serotonin and Norepinephrine.

Pristiq (Desvenlafaxine). FDA Package Insert. 02-2018.
https://www.accessdata.fda.gov/drugsatfda_docs/label/2018/021992s042lbl.pdf. Date Accessed: 7-22-2021.

9. **Answer E.** The Locus Coeruleus is involved in the creation of Norepinephrine. The Raphe Nucleus is involved in the creation of Serotonin.

Fix, James D, Brueckner, Jennifer K. High-Yield Neuroanatomy. Baltimore: Lippincott Williams & Wilkins. 2009. Pages 151-153.

Case 15

An 8 year old girl brought in for evaluation by her parents to help her relax. The patient reports that she worries about the safety of her family, worries about them getting sick and dying. Over the past year she made comments that she is concerned that her parents will be gone when she wakes up from sleep. Other things she worries about is school, she gets good grades, but she becomes really concerned if she did her work right and turned in the right work. She also reports concern about what her friends think about her. She also often thinks about conversations she has had with people in the past and if she said the wrong thing. She does have friends and is able to play with them. Lately the worries have been making it difficult for her to make decisions and she's noticed that she is having a harder time sleeping because of the worries. Sometimes she worries so much that she feels pains in her stomach.

Multiple Choice Questions:

1. What is the diagnosis or diagnoses? – Choose all answers that apply

A. Major Depressive Disorder

B. Social Anxiety Disorder

C. Panic Disorder

D. Agoraphobia

E. Generalized Anxiety Disorder

F. Somatic Disorder

G. None of the above

2. What is the estimated prevalence of this disorder in the USA in teenagers?

A. 0.5%

B. 0.6%

C. 0.7%

D. 0.8%

E. 0.9%

3. Which of the following screening scales would be most helpful in this case to quantify the severity of the patient's symptoms?

A. PHQ-9

B. CY-BOCS

C. CSSR

D. CDRS

E. CARS

F. None of the Above

4. Which of the following disorders is most closely associated with depression?

A. Social Anxiety Disorder

B. Generalized Anxiety Disorder

C. Panic Disorder

D. Agoraphobia

E. Separation Anxiety Disorder

5. Which of the following treatments would be most beneficial to the patient?

A. Exposure and Response Prevention

B. Interpersonal Psychotherapy

C. Family-Based Treatment

D. Dialectical Behavioral Therapy

E. Psychodynamic Psychotherapy

F. Coping Cat

G. None of the above

References & Answers:

1. Answer E. The patient meets criteria for Generalized Anxiety Disorder. She has several areas of worry that are impairing her life and have been making it difficult for her to sleep, make decisions, and have started to manifest as somatic pains. Although her worries do have some elements of Separation Anxiety Disorder and Social Anxiety Disorder, her group of symptoms are best categorized under Generalized Anxiety Disorder.

DSM-5. Anxiety Disorders. Generalized Anxiety Disorder. Pages 222-226.

2. Answer E. The estimated prevalence of the disorder in teenagers is 0.9%.

DSM-5. Anxiety Disorders. Generalized Anxiety Disorder. Pages 223.

3. Answer F. None of the listed options would be appropriate for exploring the patient's anxiety symptoms. A more appropriate choice would be the SCARED – Screen for Child Anxiety Related Emotional Disorders.

Assessment Scales in Child and Adolescent Psychiatry. 2006. Frank C Verhulst, MD. Jan van der Ende. Screen for Child Anxiety Related Emotional Disorders. Page 62.

Lewis's Child & Adolescent Psychiatry Textbook. 5th Edition. 2018. Chapter 5.5.1. Page 513.

4. Answer B. Out of the listed disorders. Generalized Anxiety Disorder is the most closely associated with depression.

Lewis's Child & Adolescent Psychiatry Textbook. 5th Edition. 2018. Chapter 5.5.1. Page 512.

5. Answer F. Out of the listed treatment options, Coping Cat would be the most beneficial to the patient. Coping Cat is a form of CBT that has evidence in the treatment of anxiety disorders in youth.

Lewis's Child & Adolescent Psychiatry Textbook. 5th Edition. 2018. Chapter 5.5.1. Page 514.

Beidas, R. S., et al. Flexible Applications of the Coping Cat Program for Anxious Youth. Cognitve Behavioral Practice. 2010 May 1;17(2):142-143.

Case 16

A 15 year old male presents for an evaluation for having trouble at school and making friends.

He reports that for the past 2-3 months he has stopped feeling happy. He began isolating himself and started to feel like there was no hope for him. He has a hard time going to sleep and staying asleep. He no longer seems to enjoy things like he used to like painting, playing board games, or baking with his family. He is no longer passing his classes. When asked why his grades have dropped, he reports that he cannot concentrate like he used to and has lost interest in school. For the past 3 weeks he has being having thoughts about there being no point to him being alive anymore. He has never had suicidal intent, attempts, or plans.

Prior to the problem with his mood, his parents noticed him change about 6 months ago. When they asked what was wrong, he told them that he was feeling anxious. He started to avoid being around other people at pep rallies, birthday parties, and other events because he worried about being scrutinized. He has lost several friends because of this, and his parents find this strange because he used to be very popular and made friends easily. He finds it difficult to walk down the halls of his school, since he gets concerned about being judged or doing something embarrassing. He struggles with knowing what to say to people and tends to be quiet around others. He often notices that his heart starts beating fast when around groups of people. He reports that his anxiety makes it difficult to have friends.

His Primary Care Physician started him on Escitalopram about 3 months ago and he has been on Escitalopram 20 mg daily for 8 weeks, the parents and patient do not think the medication is helping.

Multiple Choice Questions:

1. What is the diagnosis or diagnoses? – Choose all answers that apply

A. Agoraphobia

B. Bipolar Disorder

C. Disruptive Mood Dysregulation Disorder

D. Major Depressive Disorder

E. Panic Disorder

F. Social Anxiety Disorder

G. None of the above

2. Which medication would be the most appropriate next choice for the patient?

A. Citalopram

B. Fluoxetine

C. Aripiprazole

D. Lithium

E. Desvenlafaxine

F. None of the above

3. Which psychotherapy and which medication in combination have strong support for use in this case?

A. Dialectical Behavioral Therapy

B. Group Therapy

C. Cognitive Behavioral Therapy

D. Interpersonal and Social Rhythm Therapy

E. Desvenlafaxine

F. Aripiprazole

G. Citalopram

H. Fluoxetine

4. It is estimated that approximately ¾ of patients with which disorder have an age of onset between age 8 – 15 years.

A. Agoraphobia

B. Bipolar Disorder

C. Disruptive Mood Dysregulation Disorder

D. Major Depressive Disorder

E. Panic Disorder

F. Social Anxiety Disorder

G. None of the above

5. Escitalopram is approved for the usage of which disorder in adolescents?

A. Agoraphobia

B. Bipolar Disorder

C. Disruptive Mood Dysregulation Disorder

D. Major Depressive Disorder

E. Panic Disorder

F. Social Anxiety Disorder

G. None of the above

References & Answers:

1. **Answer D & F.** The patient meets criteria for Major Depressive Disorder & Social Anxiety Disorder.

DSM-5. Anxiety Disorders. Social Anxiety Disorder. Pages 202-208.

DSM-5. Depressive Disorders. Major Depressive Disorder. Pages 160-168.

2. **Answer B.** The patient has failed a trial of Escitalopram, he has been on the max dosage of Escitalopram for 2 months and reports no significant improvement in symptoms. The next best choice would be Fluoxetine.

Prozac (Fluoxetine). Package Insert. 04-2020.
https://www.accessdata.fda.gov/drugsatfda_docs/label/2020/018936s109lbl.pdf/

Date Accessed: 7-25-2021.

March, J. et al. The Treatment for Adolescents With Depression Study (TADS). Arch Gen Psychiatry. 2007;64(10):1132-1144

Brent, D. et al. Switching to Another SSRI or to Venlafaxine With or Without Cognitive Behavioral Therapy For Adolescents With SSRI-Resistant Depression. JAMA. 2008 Feb 27;299(8):901-913.

3. **Answer C & H.** Cognitive Behavioral Therapy and Fluoxetine have the strongest evidence for use in combination treatment for depression in adolescents.

Prozac (Fluoxetine). Package Insert. 04-2020.
https://www.accessdata.fda.gov/drugsatfda_docs/label/2020/018936s109lbl.pdf/

Date Accessed: 7-25-2021.

March, J. et al. The Treatment for Adolescents With Depression Study (TADS). Arch Gen Psychiatry. 2007;64(10):1132-1144

Brent, D. et al. Switching to Another SSRI or to Venlafaxine With or Without Cognitive Behavioral Therapy For Adolescents With SSRI-Resistant Depression. JAMA. 2008 Feb 27;299(8):901-913.

4. **Answer F.** It is estimated that approximately 75% (3/4) of patients with Social Anxiety Disorder have an age of onset between ages 8 – 15 years old.

DSM-5. Anxiety Disorders. Social Anxiety Disorder. Pages 205.

5. **Answer D.** Escitalopram is approved for the use in Major Depressive Disorder in Adolescents ages 12 and up.

Escitalopram. FDA Package Insert. 08-2020.
https://www.accessdata.fda.gov/drugsatfda_docs/label/2020/021323s052,021365s037lbl.pdf

Date Accessed: 7/25/2021.

Case 17

A 13 year old female presents with her mother for help with her feelings.

The patient reports that she has not been feeling like herself for almost a year. She no longer feels like life is worth living and does not feel like she can find joy in things anymore. She reports that she has felt sad in the past before, after her grandmother died, but she reports the current sadness she feels is worse than that. Her mother has noted that her daughter has a hard time controlling her feelings and has a hard time falling asleep. She has also noted that the patient has lost weight and does not eat much of her meals. About a week ago her mother heard the patient scream, "Shut up!" while the patient was in the shower. When asked about this the patient stated that everyday, she's been hearing and seeing a dark cloud that tells her bad things, this first started a few weeks ago.

Multiple Choice Questions:

1. What is the diagnosis or diagnoses? – Choose all answers that apply

A. Schizophrenia

B. Schizoaffective Disorder

C. Bipolar Disorder

D. Major Depressive Disorder

E. Schizophreniform Disorder

F. None of the above

2. Which of the following treatments would be appropriate?

A. SSRI

B. SNRI

C. Mood Stabilizer

D. Antipsychotic

E. None of the above

3. Which of the following is thought to be a significant risk factor for the disorder the patient has?

A. Sexual Abuse

B. Bullying

C. Cigarette Smoking

D. Losing a parent

E. Losing a sibling

4. Which of the following is true?

A. Hallucinations related to mood are most often auditory

B. Hallucinations related to mood are most often visual

C. Hallucinations related to mood are most often auditory & visual

D. None of the above

5. Children without frank psychotic disorders can also experience hallucinations and delusions, after what age are these experiences thought to usually diminish?

A. 9

B. 8

C. 7

D. 6

E. 5

References & Answers:

1. **Answer D.** The patient meets criteria for Major Depressive Disorder. She also has also developed psychotic symptoms because of the depression, hearing and seeing a black cloud that tells her bad things.

DSM-5. Depressive Disorders. Major Depressive Disorder. Pages 160-168, 186.

2. **Answer E.** The most appropriate treatment would be a combination of antidepressant treatment and antipsychotic treatment. Although there is a lack of research in the treatment of Major Depressive Disorder with psychotic features in children. It would be reasonable to approach the case as you would in adults with Major Depressive Disorder with psychotics features by starting antidepressant treatment and antipsychotic treatment.

Courvoisie, H. et al. Psychosis in children: diagnosis and treatment. Dialogues Clin Neurosci. 2001 Jun; 3(2): 89.

Carlson, G.A., & Pataki, C. (2020). Affective Disorders with Psychosis in Youth An Update. E.M. House & J.W. Tyson (Eds.), Psychosis in Children and Adolescents: A Guide for Clinicians (page 97). Child and Adolescent Psychiatric Clinics of North America. Volume 29, Number 1. Elsevier.

3. **Answer A.** The literature shows that sexual abuse is a significant risk factor for the development of Major Depressive Disorder with psychotic features.

Carlson, G.A., & Pataki, C. (2020). Affective Disorders with Psychosis in Youth An Update. E.M. House & J.W. Tyson (Eds.), Psychosis in Children and Adolescents: A Guide for Clinicians (page 96). Child and Adolescent Psychiatric Clinics of North America. Volume 29, Number 1. Elsevier.

4. **Answer A.** It has been noted in the literature that hallucinations related to mood are most often auditory.

Carlson, G.A., & Pataki, C. (2020). Affective Disorders with Psychosis in Youth An Update. E.M. House & J.W. Tyson (Eds.), Psychosis in Children and Adolescents: A Guide for Clinicians (page 97). Child and Adolescent Psychiatric Clinics of North America. Volume 29, Number 1. Elsevier.

5. **Answer D.** Children without frank psychotics disorders can experience transient symptoms of hallucinations and delusions, the literature notes that these experiences typically diminish after the age of

Driver, D.I., et al. (2020). Childhood-Onset Schizophrenia and Early-onset Schizophrenia Spectrum Disorders: An Update. E.M. House & J.W. Tyson (Eds.), Psychosis in Children and Adolescents: A Guide for Clinicians (page 81). Child and Adolescent Psychiatric Clinics of North America. Volume 29, Number 1. Elsevier.

Case 18

A 11 year old male presents with his parents for trouble at school.

His parents report that he started getting in trouble at school in 2nd grade. He would get easily distracted by what other children were doing in the classroom. When teachers would talk to him, he seemed to be daydreaming. He also had a hard time following along with classroom lessons. He was moved to the front of the class for his teachers to keep an eye on him. His parents do note that at home they have a hard time getting him to do work, they must sit with him to make sure he does it. He is very forgetful when given instructions and is often losing his assignments. He is also not good at keeping his backpack organized despite his parents and teachers helping him organize it. Sometimes he does get irritable with is parents when they ask him to finish his work.

Multiple Choice Questions:

1. What is the diagnosis or diagnoses? – Choose all answers that apply

A. Oppositional Defiant Disorder

B. Conduct Disorder

C. Disruptive Mood Dysregulation Disorder

D. Attention Deficit Hyperactivity Disorder

E. Developmentally Appropriate Behavior

F. None of the above

2. Which of the following treatments would be appropriate?

A. Risperidone

B. Guanfacine

C. Sertraline

D. Lithium

E. Valproic Acid

3. Which of the following can be helpful in quantifying the patient's symptoms and response to treatment ?

A. PHQ-9

B. GAD-7

C. CY-BOCS

D. Vanderbilt

E. None of the above

4. What is the estimated percentage of patients with the disorder in this case, who still experience symptoms into adulthood

A. 10%

B. 20%

C. 30%

D. 40%

E. 50%

F. 60%

G. None of the above

5. Which of the following disorders is thought to have a higher rate of comorbidity with the disorder the patient has?

A. Oppositional Defiant Disorder

B. Disruptive Mood Dysregulation Disorder

C. Major Depressive Disorder

D. Generalized Anxiety Disorder

6. Before what age must symptoms of this disorder be present to diagnosis this disorder?

A. 10

B. 11

C. 12

D. 13

E. None of the above

References & Answers:

1. **Answer D.** He meets criteria for Attention Deficit Hyperactivity Disorder, Predominantly Inattentive Presentation.

DSM-5. Neurodevelopmental Disorders. Attention Deficit Hyperactive Disorder. Pages 59-65.

2. **Answer B.** Out of the list medications, the most appropriate choice would be Guanfacine an Alpha-2 Agonist that is FDA approved for the treatment of ADHD in Children & Adolescents.

Lewis's Child & Adolescent Psychiatry Textbook. 5th Edition. 2018. Chapter 5.1.1. Page 374-376.

3. **Answer D.** Out of the listed options, the Vanderbilt form is the best choice in quantifying the patient's symptoms and response to treatment.

Dulcan, M.K. Dulcan's Textbook of Child and Adolescent Psychiatry. 2nd Edition 2016. Chapter 10. Attention Deficit Hyperactive Disorder.

4. **Answer F.** Approximately 60% of Child & Adolescent Patient's with ADHD will continue to experience ADHD symptoms into Adulthood, primarily the inattentive symptoms.

Lewis's Child & Adolescent Psychiatry Textbook. 5th Edition. 2018. Chapter 5.1.1. Page 365.

5. **Answer A.** Out of the listed disorders, Oppositional Defiant Disorder is thought to have the higher rate of comorbidity with ADHD.

Lewis's Child & Adolescent Psychiatry Textbook. 5th Edition. 2018. Chapter 5.1.1. Page 372.

6. **Answer C.** Symptoms most be present prior to the age of 12.

DSM-5. Neurodevelopmental Disorders. Attention Deficit Hyperactive Disorder. Pages 59-60.

Case 19

A 16-year-old male patient presents with his parents for concerns about him hanging out with the wrong crowd.

About a week ago he smoked a new strain of cannabis with his friends and started hearing voices. The voices tell him strange things, but he ignores them. He often skips school and does not do homework and will smoke cannabis with his friends instead. He has been arrested at school for having cannabis at school. The patient reports that his parents should just stay out of his social life. He reports that he does smoke cannabis daily and has been smoking for at least 1 year. He used to smoke 1 blunt a day but now smokes 2-3 to get high. This past week he has not been able to smoke since his parents have grounded him. His parents have noted for the past week he has not been able to sleep well, is not eating, and has been irritable with the family.

Multiple Choice Questions:

1. What is the diagnosis or diagnoses? – Choose all answers that apply

A. Substance Induced Psychotic Disorder

B. Bipolar Disorder

C. Schizophreniform Disorder

D. Schizoaffective Disorder

E. Cannabis Use Disorder

F. Schizophrenia

G. None of the above

2. It is believed that the usage of which substance is associated with an approximate doubled risk of developing an anxiety disorder?

A. Caffeine

B. Cannabis

C. Ketamine

D. Phencyclidine

3. One-time usage of Cannabis can be detected via Urinalysis for approximately how many days?

A. 1-2 Days

B. 1-3 Days

C. 1-4 Days

D. 1-5 Days

4. Which of the following is believed to be the primary psychoactive component of Cannabis?

A. Delta (9)-tetrahydrocannabinol

B. Cannabidiol

C. Lysergic acid diethylamide

D. 3,4-Methylenedioxymethamphetamine

E. None of the above

5. A few months later the patient is diagnosed with Attention Deficit Hyperactivity Disorder, which of the following treatment options is thought to have less abuse potential?

A. Methylphenidate

B. Amphetamine

C. Atomoxetine

D. Dextroamphetamine

E. Dexmethylphenidate

6. Which of the following genes has been associated with psychotic symptoms after smoking cannabis?

A. FOXP2

B. HTT

C. FMR1

D. ATP7B

E. TSC1

F. AKT1

References & Answers:

1. **Answer A & E.** The patient meets criteria for Substance Induced Psychotic Disorder – started hallucinating after smoking a new strain of cannabis. He also meets criteria for Cannabis Use Disorder, of note he is also experience Cannabis Withdrawal.

DSM-5. Schizophrenia Spectrum and Other Psychotic Disorders. Substance/Medication Induced Psychotic Disorder. Pages 110-115.

DSM-5. Substance-Related and Addictive Disorders. Cannabis Use Disorder. Pages 509-515.

2. Answer B. The usage of Cannabis is associated with an approximate double risk of developing anxiety disorders.

Dulcan, M.K. Dulcan's Textbook of Child and Adolescent Psychiatry. 2nd Edition 2016. Chapter 12. Substance Use Disorders and Addictions.

3. Answer B. One time usage of Cannabis can be detected via Urinalysis for approximately 1-3 days.

Lewis's Child & Adolescent Psychiatry Textbook. 5th Edition. 2018. Chapter 5.8. Page 575-578.

4. Answer A. The primary psychoactive component of Cannabis is believed to be Delta (9)-tetrahydrocannabinol.

Lewis's Child & Adolescent Psychiatry Textbook. 5th Edition. 2018. Chapter 5.8. Page 573

Colizzi, M., Weltens, N., McGuire, P. et al. Delta-9-tetrahydrocannabinol increases striatal glutamate levels in healthy individuals: implications for psychosis. Mol Psychiatry 25, 3231–3240 (2020). https://doi.org/10.1038/s41380-019-0374-8

5. Answer C. Atomoxetine is thought to have the least amount of abuse potential out of the listed options.

Lewis's Child & Adolescent Psychiatry Textbook. 5th Edition. 2018. Chapter 5.8. Page 576.

Dulcan, M.K. Dulcan's Textbook of Child and Adolescent Psychiatry. 2nd Edition 2016. Chapter 12. Substance Use Disorders and Addictions.

6. Answer F. AKT1 is a gene that has been associated with psychotic symptoms after smoking Cannabis.

Morgan, CJA., et al. AKT1 genotype moderates the acute psychotomimetic effects of naturalistically smoked cannabis in young cannabis smokers. Transl Psychiatry (2016) 6, e738. Page 5.

Ibarra-Lecue, I., et al. Chronic cannabis promotes pro-hallucinogenic signaling of 5-HT2A receptors through Akt/mTOR pathway. Neuropsychopharmacology (2018) 43:2028–2035. Page 2028.

Case 20

A 6-year-old who presents with his parents with behavioral problems at home and school

His parents report that for over a year now they have been receiving complaints about his behavior at school. He is constantly getting up and out of his seat without permission. He blurts out answers and interrupts his teachers. When it is quiet time and nap time in the afternoon, he will yell and scream. He constantly gets in trouble for running down the halls of the school. At home his parents have a hard time getting him to be quiet and not talk so much. They also describe him as being very impatient and that he gets distracted easily. He has also started to become oppositional and throws things when angry. His pediatrician has tried several different medications to help treat his behavior: valproic acid, clonidine, atomoxetine, dexmethylphenidate, and amphetamines. He is currently on Methylphenidate Extended Release 54 mg daily.

Multiple Choice Questions:

1. What is the diagnosis or diagnoses? – Choose all answers that apply

A. Disruptive Mood Dysregulation Disorder

B. Attention Deficit Hyperactivity Disorder

C. Bipolar Disorder

D. Major Depressive Disorder

E. Generalized Anxiety Disorder

F. None of the Above

2. Which of the following treatments would be recommended before making an adjustment to the patient's medication regimen?

A. Psychodynamic Psychotherapy

B. Interpersonal Psychotherapy

C. Dialectical Behavioral Therapy

D. Parent Management Training

E. None of the above

3. The patient has become increasingly oppositional towards everyone and physically aggressive despite an adequate trial of the treatment from Question 2, which of the following has the best evidence to be helpful in cases like this?

A. Quetiapine

B. Lithium

C. Valproic Acid

D. Risperidone

E. None of the above

4. Which of the following tools helps rate both externalizing and internalizing behaviors in children and adolescents?

A. PHQ-9

B. GAD-7

C. CAGE

D. CBCL

E. CARS

F. None of the above

5. Comorbid anxiety disorders are thought to be found in what percentage of patients like the patient in this case?

A. 5% - 10%

B. 15% - 20%

C. 20% - 25%

D. 25% - 30%

E. 30% - 35%

References & Answers:

1. Answer B. The meets criteria for Attention Deficit Hyperactivity Disorder, Predominantly Hyperactive/Impulsive Presentation.

DSM-5. Neurodevelopmental Disorders. ADHD. Page 59-65.

2. Answer D. Before making an adjustment to his medication regimen, Parent Management Training would be the best recommendation.

Lewis's Child & Adolescent Psychiatry Textbook. 5th Edition. 2018. Chapter 5.1.1. Page 374.

Dulcan, M.K. Dulcan's Textbook of Child and Adolescent Psychiatry. 2nd Edition 2016. Chapter 41.

3. Answer D. In cases where Parent Management Training and an adequate trial of stimulant ADHD medications have not been effective, the Treatment of Severe Childhood Aggression Study found that the addition of Risperidone can be of useful.

Aman, M.G., et al. What Does Risperidone Add to Parent Training and Stimulant for Severe Aggression in Child Attention-Deficit/Hyperactivity Disorder? J. Am. Acad. Child Adolesc. Psychiatry, 2014;53(1):47–60

Lewis's Child & Adolescent Psychiatry Textbook. 5th Edition. 2018. Chapter 5.1.3. Page 405.

4. Answer D. The CBCL (Child Behavioral Checklist) is a tool that help you rate the externalizing and internalizing behaviors in Children & Adolescents.

Lewis's Child & Adolescent Psychiatry Textbook. 5th Edition. 2018. Chapter 6.24. Page 800.

Frank C Verhulst, MD, Jan van der Ende. Assessment Scales in Child and Adolescent Psychiatry. Achenbach System of Empirically Based Assessment (ASEBA) – Preschool and School-Age Forms. London: Informa UK Ltd. 2006. Page 17 - 22.

5. Answer D. It is estimated that approximately 25%-30% of patients with this disorder also have comorbid anxiety disorders.

Lewis's Child & Adolescent Psychiatry Textbook. 5th Edition. 2018. Chapter 5.1.1. Page 372.

Case 21

A 16-year-old girl who presents with her parents for issues with socializing.

The parents report that since the patient was around the age of 12 she has had trouble socializing with others and making friends. The patient reports that it is hard for her to make friends and be around people. When she interacts with others, she has concerns about being viewed like she does not belong and at times feels like people are judging her. One of the reasons she feels like people might judge her is because she has Ulcerative Colitis and missed a few weeks of school in the beginning of the school year and was allowed to catch up with her assignments and keep her status as the top ranked student in her class. She was diagnosed with Ulcerative Colitis 2 years ago. Her Ulcerative Colitis symptoms have been well controlled for the past 2 months.

She is currently taking Mercaptopurine 50 mg daily and Fluticasone Intranasal (1-2 sprays a day).

Multiple Choice Questions:

1. What is the diagnosis or diagnoses? – Choose all answers that apply

A. Adjustment Disorder

B. Panic Disorder

C. Agoraphobia

D. Generalized Anxiety Disorder

E. Social Anxiety Disorder

F. None of the Above

2. Which of the following classes of medications would be the most appropriate choice for this patient's disorder?

A. SNRI

B. SSRI

C. Antipsychotic

D. Lithium

E. TCA

F. None of the Above

3. In children with Chronic Medical Conditions like the patient in this case, which of the following is likely?

A. Higher Prevalence of Anxiety Disorders compared to the general population

B. Lower Prevalence of Anxiety Disorders compared to the general population

C. Prevalence of Anxiety Disorders is the same compared to the general population

D. Prevalence cannot be measured

E. None of the above

4. Which of the following psychiatric medications is contraindicated when using Mercaptopurine?

A. Sertraline

B. Duloxetine

C. Citalopram

D. Melatonin

E. Venlafaxine

F. None of the above

5. A few months pass and the patient has responded well to the treatment chosen in question 2, however you receive labs results back from the patient indicating low number of Leukocytes. The patient is taking is still taking Mercaptopurine 50 mg daily, Fluticasone Intranasal, in addition to the treatment chosen in question 2. Which medication is likely the cause of the lab abnormality?

A. Mercaptopurine

B. Fluticasone

C. SNRI

D. SSRI

E. Antipsychotic

F. Lithium

G. TCA

F. None of the Above

References & Answers:

1. **Answer E.** The patient meets criteria for Social Anxiety Disorder.

DSM-5. Anxiety Disorders. Social Anxiety Disorder. Page 202-208.

2. **Answer B.** SSRI (Selective Serotonin Reuptake Inhibitors) is the most appropriate choice in medication treatment options for anxiety disorders in Children & Adolescents.

Walkup, J. et al. Cognitive Behavioral Therapy, Sertraline, or a Combination in Childhood Anxiety. N Engl J Med 2008;359:2753-66.

Lewis's Child & Adolescent Psychiatry Textbook. 5th Edition. 2018. Chapter 5.5.1. Page 515.

3. **Answer A.** Children with Chronic Medical Conditions are more likely to have a higher Prevalence of Anxiety Disorders compared to the general population.

Cobham, V.E., et al. Systematic Review: Anxiety in Children and Adolescents With Chronic Medical Conditions. J Am Acad Child Adolesc Psychiatry 2020;59(5):595–618. Page 595, 614.

4. **Answer F.** None of the psychiatric medications listed are contraindicated to be used in conjunction with Mercaptopurine.

Mercaptopurine. FDA Package Insert. 04-2014.

https://www.accessdata.fda.gov/drugsatfda_docs/label/2014/205919s000lbl.pdf

Date Accessed: 02-26-2021

5. **Answer A.** The most likely cause of the lab abnormality is Mercaptopurine, since Mercaptopurine is an immunosuppressant.

Mercaptopurine. FDA Package Insert. 04-2014.

https://www.accessdata.fda.gov/drugsatfda_docs/label/2014/205919s000lbl.pdf

Date Accessed: 02-26-2021

Case 22

A 7 year old boy brought in by his parent for help with his worries. The parent reports that the patient is constantly worried that something bad might happen to his parents if he is not with them. It has reached a point where he's been refusing to go to school. The boy says that he needs to make sure his parents are safe by staying home with them. He has not been to school for about a month. The last time he went to school his father had to force him out of the car. After being in school for about one hour, he ran home. He has been invited to sleep overs with his friends, but he has been refusing to go. The parent cannot recall an event that could of triggered his current behavior but believes it started about two months ago.

Multiple Choice Questions:

1. What is the diagnosis or diagnoses? – Choose all answers that apply

A. Generalized Anxiety Disorder

B. Panic Disorder

C. Social Anxiety Disorder

D. Separation Anxiety Disorder

E. None of the above

2. Which of the following treatments would be most appropriate?

A. Interpersonal Therapy

B. Dialectical Behavioral Therapy

C. Coping Cat

D. Psychodynamic Therapy

E. None of the above

3. 2 months pass and the parents report that the patient is still having difficulty going to school. Which of the following treatment options would be the most appropriate choice?

A. Escitalopram

B. Fluoxetine

C. Duloxetine

D. Venlafaxine

E. Sertraline

4. The disorder the patient has is thought to be the prevalent disorder of its class in which age group?

A. < 4 years of age

B. < 6 years of age

C. < 8 years of age

D. < 10 years of age

E. < 12 years of age

5. What is the time frame need to diagnosis this disorder in children and adults?

A. 1 week in children, 2 months in adults

B. 2 weeks in children, 3 months in adults

C. 3 weeks in children, 4 months in adults

D. 4 weeks in children, 5 months in adults

E. None of the above

References & Answers:

1.**Answer D.** The patient meets the criteria for Separation Anxiety Disorder.

DSM-5. Anxiety Disorders. Separation Anxiety Disorder. Pages 190-195.

2. **Answer C.** Coping Cat is a form of Cognitive Behavioral Therapy that has been shown to be helpful in the treatment of anxiety disorders such as Separation Anxiety Disorder, Social Anxiety Disorder, and Generalized Anxiety Disorder.

Lewis's Child & Adolescent Psychiatry Textbook. 5th Edition. 2018. Chapter 5.5.1. Page 514.

Beidas, R. S., et al. Flexible Applications of the Coping Cat Program for Anxious Youth. Cognitve Behavioral Practice. 2010 May 1;17(2):142-143.

3. **Answer E.** If treatment with Coping Cat or Cognitive Behavioral Therapy is not effective, the addition of an SSRI like Sertraline is reasonable.

Lewis's Child & Adolescent Psychiatry Textbook. 5th Edition. 2018. Chapter 5.5.1. Page 515.

4. **Answer E.** Separation Anxiety Disorder is thought to be the most prevalent anxiety disorder in ages less than 12.

DSM-5. Anxiety Disorders. Separation Anxiety Disorder. Pages 190-195.

5. **Answer E.** The time frame of diagnosis in children with this disorder is 4 weeks, the time frame of diagnosis in adults with this disorder is 6 months.

DSM-5. Anxiety Disorders. Separation Anxiety Disorder. Pages 190-195.

Case 23

A 15 year old female who presents with her parents about stress at home and school.

The patient's parents report that the patient often gets teased at school because she dresses more like a teenage boy rather than a teenage girl. She recently got into a physical altercation with a girl in her class because of a vulgar word the girl said to the patient. The patient and the girl both got suspended because of the fight. The patient reports that she has always identified more with being a boy rather than a girl. A few years ago, she started dressing more a like a boy because she does not like girl clothes. She prefers to be addressed as a boy and has asked her family and friends to address her as Rob instead of her birth name Roberta. She has cried in the past because she wishes she could become a boy. She reports its frustrating living in a world that does not understand her. A few weeks ago, she scratched her arm with a paper clip after having an argument with her parents about wanting to be called Rob.

Multiple Choice Questions:

1. What is the diagnosis or diagnoses? – Choose all answers that apply

A. Major Depressive Disorder

B. Social Anxiety Disorder

C. Transvestic Disorder

D. Borderline Personality Disorder

E. None of the above

2. What is the minimum number of required symptoms of the disorder the patient has if they were a child?

A. 2

B. 3

C. 4

D. 5

E. 6

F. None of the above

3. Which of the following is accurate?

A. Persistence of the disorder the patient has from childhood to adolescence is high

B. Persistence of the disorder the patient has from childhood to adolescence is low

C. Persistence of the disorder the patient has from adolescence to adulthood is equal to that of childhood to adolescence.

D. None of the above

4. It is believed that children have a sense of gender identity by what age?

A. 1

B. 2

C. 3

D. 4

E. 5

5. Treatment with which of the following and at what Tanner stage could you consider starting treatment to suppress puberty in patients with this disorder?

A. GnRH & Tanner Stage 1

B. GnRH & Tanner Stage 2

C. FSH & Tanner Stage 1

D. LH & Tanner Stage 2

E. None of the above

6. LGBT youth are thought to have:

A. Higher rates of suicidal ideation than non LGBT youth

B. Lower rates of suicidal ideation than non LGBT youth

C. Rate of suicidal ideation in LGBT youth is the same as non LGBT youth

D. None of the above

References & Answers:

1. Answer E. The patient meets the diagnostic criteria for Gender Dysphoria.

DSM-5. Gender Dysphoria. Pages 451-459. Page 452.

2. Answer E. If this patient were a child they must have at least 6 symptoms of Gender Dysphoria in order to be able to meet criteria for the diagnosis. In adolescents you must have at least 2 symptoms.

DSM-5. Gender Dysphoria. Pages 451-459. Page 452.

3. Answer B. It is believed that the persistence of Gender Dysphoria from childhood to adolescents is low. The persistence of Gender Dysphoria from adolescence to adulthood is higher.

Lewis's Child & Adolescent Psychiatry Textbook. 5th Edition. 2018. Chapter 5.14. Page 638.

4. Answer C. It is believed that children develop a sense of gender identity by age 3.

Dulcan, M.K. Dulcan's Textbook of Child and Adolescent Psychiatry. 2nd Edition 2016. Chapter 28. (Key Concepts and Terminology)

5. Answer B. In order to suppress puberty in patients with this disorder, it would require treatment with GnRH and can be considered once a patient is at Tanner Stage 2.

Dulcan, M.K. Dulcan's Textbook of Child and Adolescent Psychiatry. 2nd Edition 2016. Chapter 28. (Pubertal suppression).

6. Answer A. Rates of suicidal ideation are higher in LGBT youth than non-LGBT youth.

Dulcan, M.K. Dulcan's Textbook of Child and Adolescent Psychiatry. 2nd Edition 2016. Chapter 28. (Mental Health Vulnerabilities for LGBT Youth).

Case 24

A 16 year old male recently out on bail, a judge ordered his parents bring him for a psychiatric evaluation.

His parents report that two years ago his doctor prescribed him with Lorazepam 0.5 mg daily for anxiety as needed. At first the patient only used it about once a week but over time he started taking it every day and uses it multiple times a day to keep calm. He is out on bail for having Alprazolam at school and trying to sell it to a fellow student. He reports that he was just holding it for friend. Sometimes he has used Alprazolam in addition to his Lorazepam to help keep himself calm when Lorazepam is not working and when he feels shaky. He likes using these medications and is not interested in stopping.

Multiple Choice Questions:

1. What is the diagnosis or diagnoses? – Choose all answers that apply

A. Major Depressive Disorder

B. Alcohol Use Disorder

C. Generalized Anxiety Disorder

D. Benzodiazepine Use Disorder

E. Substance Induced Mood Disorder

F. None of the above

2. Among 12 – 17 year olds this disorder is highest among which group?

A. African American

B. Hispanic

C. Native American

D. Asian American & Pacific Islanders

E. None of the above

3. Which of the following is true in the context of therapeutic use of benzodiazepines?

A. Pediatric patients need larger mg/kg doses of benzodiazepines

B. Pediatric patients need smaller mg/kg doses of benzodiazepines

C. Pediatric patients' dosages of benzodiazepines are the same as adults

D. None of the above

4. Studies of Benzodiazepines in Pediatric Anxiety Disorders have been:

A. Positive with sufficient power

B. Negative with sufficient power

C. Negative but underpowered

D. Positive but underpowered

E. None of the above

5. Which of the following would have been an appropriate alternative to the Benzodiazepine in this case?

A. Citalopram

B. Duloxetine

C. Quetiapine

D. Thorazine

E. Amitriptyline

References & Answers:

1. **Answer D.** The patient meets the criteria for Benzodiazepine Use Disorder.

DSM-5. Substance-Related and Addictive Disorders. Sedative, Hypnotic, or Anxiolytic Use Disorder. Pages 550-556.

2. **Answer E.** This disorder is highest among whites (0.3%) in the 12 – 17 age group.

DSM-5. Substance-Related and Addictive Disorders. Sedative, Hypnotic, or Anxiolytic Use Disorder. Pages 550-556. 553.

3. **Answer A.** Pediatric patients need larger mg/kg doses of benzodiazepines.

Chugani et al. Postnatal maturation of human $GABA_A$ receptors measured with positron emission tomography. Annals of Neurology 2001;49(5)618–26.

4. **Answer C.** There have been studies of the use Benzodiazepines in Pediatric Anxiety Disorders, but the studies have been negative and underpowered.

Lewis's Child & Adolescent Psychiatry Textbook. 5th Edition. 2018. Chapter 5.5.1. Page 515.

Kuang, H., et al. The efficacy of benzodiazepines as acute anxiolytics in children: A meta-analysis Depress Anxiety. 2017;34:888–896. Page 893.

5. **Answer B.** Out of the listed options Duloxetine would be the most appropriate choice, Duloxetine does have an indication for the treatment of anxiety in children ages 7 and up, while the other options do not.

Duloxetine (Cymbalta). FDA Package Insert. 04/2020.
https://www.accessdata.fda.gov/drugsatfda_docs/label/2020/021427s052lbl.pdf

Date Accessed: 7-25-2021.

Case 25

A 10-year-old boy who is brought in by his parent for his behavior at home and school.

Two years ago, the patient started having a hard time staying seated in class. He would often get up and out of his seat. He would disrupt his classmates and talk too much. His teacher would call at least two times a week about his behavior: interrupting others, blurting out answers, and not being able to be quiet during reading time. At home his parents report that he will run around the house despite being told not to run around so much. He is also very impatient. He screams at them when they tell him to calm down and sometimes will throw things when he does not get his way. His Pediatrician started him on Methylphenidate Extended Release 5 months ago and has been on the max dose for 3 days, the parents have noted an improvement his behavior. He had a liver transplant 3 years ago and has been on Tacrolimus since then.

Multiple Choice Questions:

1. What is the diagnosis or diagnoses? – Choose all answers that apply

A. Disruptive Mood Dysregulation Disorder

B. Intermittent Explosive Disorder

C. Bipolar Disorder

D. Major Depressive Disorder

E. None of the Above

2. Patient follows up one month later and his symptoms are not optimally controlled but the parent does not want to switch to a different medication. Which of the following medications could you add on as an adjunctive to this patient's treatment to help better control his symptoms?

A. Guanfacine Extended Release

B. Haloperidol

C. Bupropion

D. Klonopin

E. Sertraline

F. None of the above

3. The parent calls you 2 weeks later asking about non medication options for the patient's disorder, which of the following is approved for the treatment of this disorder in Children & Adolescents?

A. Transcranial Magnetic Stimulation

B. Electroconvulsive therapy

C. Dialectical Behavioral Therapy

D. Transcutaneous Electrical Nerve Stimulator via Trigeminal Nerve Stimulation

E. None of the above

4. What interactions have been identified between Tacrolimus & Methylphenidate?

A. Tacrolimus increases the levels of Methylphenidate

B. Tacrolimus decreases the levels of Methylphenidate

C. Methylphenidate increases the levels of Tacrolimus

D. Methylphenidate decreases the levels of Tacrolimus

E. None of the above

5. The patient's parent calls you after reading that hepatotoxicity could be a side effect of Methylphenidate and is worried. Which of the following is true regarding hepatoxicity in the context of oral methylphenidate use?

A. Self-Limited and Resolves Slowly

B. Self-Limited and Resolves Rapidly

C. Chronic and does not resolve

D. Chronic and resolves with treatment

E. None of the above

References & Answers:

1. **Answer E.** The patient meets the criteria for ADHD.

DSM-5. Neurodevelopmental Disorders. ADHD. Page 59-65.

2. **Answer A.** Out of the listed options, the most appropriate choice to be used as an adjunctive treatment is Guanfacine Extended Release.

Guanfacine FDA Package Insert. 02/2013.
https://www.accessdata.fda.gov/drugsatfda_docs/label/2013/022037s009lbl.pdf. Date Accessed: 03-03-2021.

3. **Answer D.** The Transcutaneous Electrical Nerve Stimulator via Trigeminal Nerve Stimulation is FDA approved for the use of treatment of ADHD in Children & Adolescents.

FDA Letter: https://www.accessdata.fda.gov/cdrh_docs/pdf18/DEN180041.pdf. Date Accessed: 03-03-2021.

FDA News Release: https://www.fda.gov/news-events/press-announcements/fda-permits-marketing-first-medical-device-treatment-adhd. Date Accessed: 03-03-2021.

4. **Answer E.** Tacrolimus and Methylphenidate have no know interactions.

Uptodate Interaction Checker. Date Accessed: 03-03-2021.

5. **Answer B.** If Hepatoxicity does occur in the context of Methylphenidate use, it is usually self-limited and resolves rapidly.

LiverTox: Clinical and Research Information on Drug-Induced Liver Injury [Internet]. Bethesda (MD): National Institute of Diabetes and Digestive and Kidney Diseases; 2012-. Methylphenidate. [Updated 2020 Feb 3]. Available from: https://www.ncbi.nlm.nih.gov/books/NBK547941/. Date Accessed:03-2-2021.

Case 26

You are consulted to evaluate an 8 year old boy on the Pediatric Inpatient Unit. He has a reported psychiatric history of Disruptive Mood Dysregulation Disorder and Attention Deficit Hyperactivity Disorder. His home medications are Lithium 150 mg twice a day, Methylphenidate 20 mg twice a day, and Clonidine 0.1 mg at bedtime. His parents brought him to the hospital for odd behavior that started about a week ago. He started to stumble around at home and school and was bumping into furniture. He reported that he saw aliens and believed he was on a spaceship. His hands were very shaky, was confusing daytime with nighttime, and was not able to respond appropriately to conversations. At times it seemed like he was back to his usual self but then after a few hours would start acting odd again. They took him to an urgent care one day before taking him to the hospital, the urgent care provider prescribed him with Risperidone 0.25 mg qhs and ordered an Intramuscular shot of Haloperidol 5 mg after he hit a staff member.

Multiple Choice Questions:

1. What is the diagnosis or diagnoses? – Choose all answers that apply

A. Major Depressive Disorder

B. Disruptive Mood Dysregulation Disorder

C. Schizoaffective Disorder

D. Bipolar Disorder, Manic Episode

E. None of the above

2. His parents report that 1 day prior to his odd behavior, he had a stomach virus and had vomited a few times. They continued to give him his scheduled medications. With this additional information, what is the likely cause of the patient's presentation?

A. Lithium

B. Haloperidol

C. Clonidine

D. Risperidone

E. None of the above

3. Which of the following could be caused by Lithium?

A. Hypothyroidism

B. Hyperthyroidism

C. Lymphocytopenia

D. SIADH

E. None of the Above

4. Which of the following is accurate?

A. Lithium circulates bound to plasma proteins

B. Lithium is 70%-80% reabsorbed by the Distal Convoluted Tubule

C. Lithium Levels Increase as Sodium Levels Decrease

D. NSAIDs cause an acute decrease in Lithium Levels

E. None of the Above

5. Which of the following is accurate?

A. Approximate half-life of Lithium in Children is 24 hours

B. Approximate half-life of Lithium in Children is 18 hours

C. Approximate half-life of Lithium in Children is 12 hours

D. Approximate half-life of Lithium in Children is 6 hours

E. None of the Above

References & Answers:

1. Answer E. The patient meets criteria for Delirium.

DSM-5. Neurocognitive Disorders. Delirium. Page 596-601.

2. Answer A. He likely has Lithium-induced Delirium. It is likely he became dehydrated from the vomiting he had from the stomach virus and became Lithium toxic since his parents continued to give him his medications. The reported shakiness, bumping into furniture, and reported confusion are likely from the Lithium toxicity.

Lewis's Child & Adolescent Psychiatry Textbook. 5th Edition. 2018. Chapter 6.1.4. Page 741-744.

3. Answer A. Hypothyroidism is a side effect that Lithium can cause, it is important to get baseline and follow up TSH levels when treating a patient with Lithium.

Rosen, M.S., et al. Lithium in Child and Adolescent Bipolar Disorder. The American Journal of Psychiatry Residents' Journal. Published Online:10 Feb 2017https://doi.org/10.1176/appi.ajp-rj.2017.120202

4. Answer C. A decrease in Sodium levels will cause an increase in Lithium Levels. Lithium is filtered out by the kidney by attaching to Sodium. Medications that effect Sodium Levels will also impact Lithium Levels, for example NSAIDs and Thiazides Diuretics.

Rosen, M.S., et al. Lithium in Child and Adolescent Bipolar Disorder. The American Journal of Psychiatry Residents' Journal. Published Online:10 Feb 2017https://doi.org/10.1176/appi.ajp-rj.2017.120202

Lewis's Child & Adolescent Psychiatry Textbook. 5th Edition. 2018. Chapter 6.1.4. Page 742-744.

5. Answer B. The approximate half-life of Lithium in Children is 18 hours. In adults the half-life is 24 hours. This is important to know because it means that in approximately 4 days you can draw a Lithium Level in Children.

Lewis's Child & Adolescent Psychiatry Textbook. 5th Edition. 2018. Chapter 6.1.4. Page 742-744.

Case 27

An 11-year-old girl is brought in for evaluation by her foster parents. Her foster parents report that the patient's mother binge drank throughout her pregnancy with the patient. When she was three years old the doctors told the foster parents that she had a condition that fell under the category of Fetal Alcohol Spectrum Disorder. Her foster parents are concerned about her ability to pay attention. She often gets in trouble for daydreaming in class. She gets distracted easily and is very forgetful. Her teachers and parents have tried several ways to help her keep her backpack organized but she constantly has trouble keeping it organized. She has a hard time following instructions and constantly losing things at home and school. The patient reports that she has a hard time paying attention to her parents and teachers, she does not know why. Recent testing at school showed that her intelligence was close to average.

Multiple Choice Questions:

1. What is the diagnosis or diagnoses? – Choose all answers that apply

A. Major Depressive Disorder

B. Attention Deficit Hyperactivity Disorder

C. Bipolar Disorder

D. Disruptive Mood Dysregulation Disorder

E. Panic Disorder

E. None of the Above

2. What is the estimated prevalence of Fetal Alcohol Spectrum Disorder worldwide?

A. 0.55%

B. 0.66%

C. 0.77%

D. 0.88%

E. 0.99%

3. How many drinks is considered binge drinking in men and women?

A. 5 or more drinks for men, 4 or more drinks in women

B. 4 or more drinks in men, 3 or more drinks in women

C. 3 or more drinks in men, 2 or more drinks in women

D. 2 or more drinks in men, 1 or more drinks in women

E. None of the above

4. Which of the following is a common characteristic in Fetal Alcohol Spectrum Disorder?

A. Long palpebral fissures, smooth philtrum, and a thick upper lip vermilion

B. Short palpebral fissures, smooth philtrum, and a thick upper lip vermilion

C. Short palpebral fissures, rough philtrum, and a thick upper lip vermilion

D. Long palpebral fissures, rough philtrum, and a thin upper lip vermilion

E. None of the above

5. When patients with Fetal Alcohol Spectrum Disorder become young adults what is the most common comorbid diagnosis?

A. Panic Disorder

B. Attention Deficit Hyperactivity Disorder

C. Major Depressive Disorder

D. Generalized Anxiety Disorder

E. None of the Above

6. The prevalence of intellectual impairment is increased by how many times in Fetal Alcohol Spectrum Disorder?

A. 94 times

B. 95 times

C. 96 times

D. 97 times

E. None of the above

7. Using DSM-5 nomenclature how might you describe Fetal Alcohol Spectrum Disorder?

A. Substance Induced Major Neurocognitive Disorder

B. Substance Induced Mild Neurocognitive Disorder

C. Major Neurocognitive Disorder

D. Mild Neurocognitive Disorder

E. Unspecified Neurocognitive Disorder

F. None of the Above

References & Answers:

1. **Answer B.** The patient meets the criteria for ADHD.

DSM-5. Neurodevelopmental Disorders. Attention Deficit Hyperactivity Disorder. Page 59-65.

2. **Answer C.** The estimated prevalence of Fetal Alcohol Spectrum Disorder is 0.77% worldwide.

Wozniak, J.R., et al. Clinical presentation, diagnosis, and management of fetal alcohol spectrum disorder. Lancet Neurol 2019; 18: 760.

3. **Answer A.** 5 or more drinks for men, 4 or more drinks in women is considered binge drinking.

Wozniak, J.R., et al. Clinical presentation, diagnosis, and management of fetal alcohol spectrum disorder. Lancet Neurol 2019; 18: 761.

4. **Answer E.** Common characteristics of Fetal Alcohol Spectrum Disorder are: flattened (smooth) philtrum, thin upper lip, short palpebral fissures

Wozniak, J.R., et al. Clinical presentation, diagnosis, and management of fetal alcohol spectrum disorder. Lancet Neurol 2019; 18: 761.

5. **Answer B.** ADHD is the most common comorbid diagnosis of Fetal Alcohol Spectrum Disorder.

Dörrie, N., et al. Fetal Alcohol Spectrum Disorders. Eur Child Adolesc Psychiatry (2014) 23:870.

6. **Answer D.** The prevalence of intellectual impairment is increased by 97 times in Fetal Alcohol Spectrum Disorder.

Wozniak, J.R., et al. Clinical presentation, diagnosis, and management of fetal alcohol spectrum disorder. Lancet Neurol 2019; 18: 765.

7. **Answer F.** Neurodevelopmental Disorder associated with Prenatal Alcohol Exposure

DSM-5. Neurodevelopmental Disorders. Other Neurodevelopmental Disorders. Page 86.

Dörrie, N., et al. Fetal Alcohol Spectrum Disorders. Eur Child Adolesc Psychiatry (2014) 23:865.

Case 28

A 15-year-old girl presents for evaluation with her parents. Her parents are concerned that she is not getting better after being on medication for depression. She was diagnosed with Major Depressive Disorder 4 months ago and has been on Fluoxetine for about 4 months as well. She was diagnosed with Major Depressive Disorder after not being able to feel like herself after surviving a fire at school 6 months ago. The patient reports that she does not feel like she will ever be able to experience happiness again. She reports that she has constant nightmares about being trapped in a burning building. She has not been to school since the incident and avoids that part of town. She is unable to recall how she was able to escape the fire. Her parents note that she startles very easily now and is overly attentive to her surroundings. She is currently on Fluoxetine 20 mg daily.

Multiple Choice Questions:

1. What is the diagnosis or diagnoses? – Choose all answers that apply

A. Major Depressive Disorder

B. Depersonalization Disorder

C. Paranoid Personality Disorder

D. Bipolar Disorder

E. Disruptive Mood Dysregulation Disorder

F. None of the Above

2. What is the estimated prevalence of this disorder in adolescents?

A. 5.7%

B. 4.7%

C. 3.7%

D. 2.7%

E. 1.7%

3. Which of the following treatments would be appropriate for the patient?

A. Dialectical Behavioral Therapy

B. Psychoanalysis

C. Psychological Debriefing

D. Trauma Focused Psychotherapy

E. None of the above

4. At what age is the criteria for this disorder different than for adults?

A. ≤12

B. ≤11

C. ≤10

D. ≤9

E. ≤8

F. None of the above

5. Which of the following medications is FDA approved for this disorder in the patient's age group?

A. Sertraline

B. Citalopram

C. Fluoxetine

D. Venlafaxine

E. Paroxetine

F. None of the above

6. Which of the following scales has been validated specifically for this disorder?

A. PHQ-9

B. GAD-7

C. SCARED

D. Vanderbilt

E. None of the Above

References & Answers:

1. **Answer F.** The patient meets criteria for PTSD rather than Major Depressive Disorder based on the available history.

DSM-5. Trauma-and Stressor-Related Disorder. Post-Traumatic Stress Disorder. Pages 271-280.

2. **Answer B.** The estimated prevalence of PTSD in adolescents is 4.7%

Lewis's Child & Adolescent Psychiatry Textbook. 5th Edition. 2018. Chapter 5.15.2. Page 651-656-658. Page 654.

3. **Answer D.** Trauma Focused Therapy would be the most appropriate therapy for the patient such as Trauma Focused Cognitive Behavioral Therapy.

Lewis's Child & Adolescent Psychiatry Textbook. 5th Edition. 2018. Chapter 5.15.2. Page 651-656-658. Page 656.

4. **Answer F.** ≤6 years old

DSM-5. Trauma-and Stressor-Related Disorder. Post-Traumatic Stress Disorder. Pages 271-280.

5. **Answer F.** There is no FDA approved medication currently that is FDA approved for the treatment of PTSD in Children or Adolescents.

Lewis's Child & Adolescent Psychiatry Textbook. 5th Edition. 2018. Chapter 5.15.2. Page 651-656-658. Page 656.

6. **Answer E.** Examples of well-known and validated scales for this disorder in children: UCLA PTSD-RI, Trauma Symptom Checklist for Young Children, and the Trauma Symptom Checklist for Children.

Lewis's Child & Adolescent Psychiatry Textbook. 5th Edition. 2018. Chapter 5.15.2. Page 651-656-658. Page 654.

Case 29

A 6 year old boy brought in by his parents for concerns about his behavior. For the past year the parents have noted that he will have moments where he wakes up from sleep, then screams and will seem frightened. His heart beats very fast during these moments. These moments happen about two times a week. Nothing seems to help calm him down during these times. When asked about this the patient reports that he does not remember this happening. Since these moments have happened at sleep overs with friends, he gets less sleep over invites and some children try to avoid him now.

Multiple Choice Questions:

1. What is the diagnosis or diagnoses? – Choose all answers that apply

A. Nightmare Disorder

B. Non-Rapid Eye Movement Sleep Arousal Disorders

C. Rapid Eye Movement Sleep Behavior Disorder

D. Narcolepsy

E. None of the Above

2. Sleep states are divided into how many main categories?

A. 1

B. 2

C. 3

D. 4

E. 5

3. Which age range is this disorder usually seen in?

A. 2 – 12 years of age

B. 3 – 12 year of age

C. 4 – 12 years of age

D. 5 – 12 year of age

4. At which stage of sleep does this disorder occur?

A. N1

B. N2

C. N3

D. REM

5. How long do the episodes of this disorder usually last?

A. 30s – 1 min

B. 30s – 2 min

C. 30s – 3 min

D. 30s – 4 min

E. 30s – 5 min

6. Which of the following statements is the most appropriate to tell the parents?

A. Inform the parent that the condition usually persists into adulthood and is benign

B. Inform the parent that the condition usually persists into adulthood and is not benign

C. Inform the parent that the condition is usually benign and rarely continues into adulthood

D. Inform the parent that the condition is usually not benign and rarely continues into adulthood

E. None of the above

References & Answers:

1. **Answer B.** The patient meets the criteria for NREM Sleep Terror Type.

DSM-5. Sleep-Wake Disorders. Non-Rapid Eye Movement Sleep Arousal Disorders. Pages 399-404.

2. **Answer B.** There are 2 main stages of sleep: NREM and REM

Lewis's Child & Adolescent Psychiatry Textbook. 5th Edition. 2018. Chapter 5.9. Page 581.

3. **Answer C.** This disorder is usually seen in between ages 4-12.

Gigliotti, F, Esposito, D, Basile, C, Cesario, S, Bruni, O. Sleep terrors—A parental nightmare. Pediatric Pulmonology. 2021; 1– 10. https://doi.org/10.1002/ppul.25304

4. **Answer C.** The disorder usually occurs at the N3 stage of sleep.

Gigliotti, F, Esposito, D, Basile, C, Cesario, S, Bruni, O. Sleep terrors—A parental nightmare. Pediatric Pulmonology. 2021; 1– 10. https://doi.org/10.1002/ppul.25304

5. **Answer E.** The episodes usually last 30 seconds to 5 minutes.

Gigliotti, F, Esposito, D, Basile, C, Cesario, S, Bruni, O. Sleep terrors—A parental nightmare. Pediatric Pulmonology. 2021; 1– 10. https://doi.org/10.1002/ppul.25304

6. **Answer C.** The most appropriate response is: Inform the parent that the condition is usually benign and rarely continues into adulthood.

Gigliotti, F, Esposito, D, Basile, C, Cesario, S, Bruni, O. Sleep terrors—A parental nightmare. Pediatric Pulmonology. 2021; 1– 10. https://doi.org/10.1002/ppul.25304

Case 30

A 9 year old boy who presents with his parents for problems with his behavior. He is currently being treated for ADHD with Methylphenidate Extended Release 36 mg daily. They report that he has been doing well academically since starting the medication one year ago. However, he got in trouble for pushing a classmate. When asked about this the patient reports that a classmate made fun of him because sometimes, he makes noises he can not control. His parents report that he has been doing that since he was in Kindergarten and blinks his eyes too much.

Multiple Choice Questions:

1. What is the diagnosis or diagnoses? – Choose all answers that apply

A. Disruptive Mood Dysregulation Disorder

B. Major Depressive Disorder

C. Social Anxiety Disorder

D. Stereotypic Movement Disorder

E. None of the Above

2. What is the typical age of onset of this disorder?

A. 2-4 years of age

B. 4-6 years of age

C. 6-8 years of age

D. 8-10 years of age

E. None of the above

3. Which of the following treatments would be appropriate for this patient?

A. CBIT

B. DBT

C. CBT

D. EMDR

E. None of the above

4. The patient's parent calls after a friend told them they should not have their child on ADHD medication because ADHD medications could make their condition worse. What would be the most appropriate thing to tell them?

A. Current evidence shows that there is an association of stimulant ADHD medications making the condition worse

B. Current evidence shows that there is no association of stimulant ADHD medications making the condition worse

C. Current evidence shows that there is an association of non-stimulant ADHD medications making the condition worse

D. Current evidence shows that there is no association of non-stimulant ADHD medications making the condition worse

E. None of the above

5. What is the peak age of severity of this disorder?

A. 6 – 8 years of age
B. 8 – 10 years of age
C. 10 – 12 year of age
D. 12 – 14 years of age
E. None of the above

6. Which medication would be the most appropriate first step treatment option if the patient's condition requires medication and you want to minimize the possibility of metabolic side effects?

A. Risperidone

B. Aripiprazole

C. Haloperidol

D. Clonidine

E. None of the above

References & Answers:

1. **Answer E.** The patient meets the criteria for Tourette's Disorder.

DSM-5. Neurodevelopmental Disorder. Tic Disorders. Pages 81-85.

2. **Answer B.** The typical age of onset of this disorder is between the ages of 4 – 6 years old.

DSM-5. Neurodevelopmental Disorder. Tic Disorders. Pages 81-85.

3. **Answer A.** The most appropriate choice would be CBIT (Comprehensive Behavioral Interventions for Tics).

Lewis's Child & Adolescent Psychiatry Textbook. 5th Edition. 2018. Chapter 6.2.2. Page757-787. Page 780.

4. **Answer B.** Current evidence shows that there is no association of stimulant ADHD medications making the condition worse

Cohen, S., et al. Meta-Analysis: Risk of Tics Associated with Stimulant Use in Randomized, Placebo-Controlled Trials. JAACAP; 2015; 54 (9); 728-736.

5. **Answer C.** The peak age of severity of this disorder is between the ages of 10 – 12 years old.

DSM-5. Neurodevelopmental Disorder. Tic Disorders. Pages 81-85.

6. **Answer D.** Clonidine would be the most appropriate treatment choice; it is an alpha 2 agonist.

Lewis's Child & Adolescent Psychiatry Textbook. 5th Edition. 2018. Chapter 5.6. Page757-787. Page 534 - 548. Page 544-545.

Murphy, T., et al. Practice Parameter for the Assessment and Treatment of Children and Adolescents With Tic Disorders. J. Am. Acad. Child Adolesc. Psychiatry, 2013; 52 (12): 1341 – 1359.

Case 31

A 17 year old girl on Lurasidone 60 mg daily presents to your office with her parents. Her parents report that the patient was started on Lurasidone about 1 year ago. 2 years ago, they noticed her behavior change. She reported she was hearing and seeing aliens, she stopped changing her clothes, at times she was incoherent, and she reported aliens had implanted a tracking device in her arm. About one to two months later she became sad, she made comments about not wanting to live anymore, seemed to be moving in slow motion, and had trouble staying asleep. The patient reports that she also remembers feeling like she had no energy and felt hopeless. She tried psychotherapy for 1 year but had no improvement, so her previous doctor started her on Lurasidone. Overall, the patient and parent report that she is doing much better and are pleased with her current medication regimen.

Multiple Choice Questions:

1. What is the diagnosis or diagnoses? – Choose all answers that apply

A. Major Depressive Disorder with Psychotic Features

B. Bipolar Disorder, most recent episode depressed, with psychotic features

C. Schizophrenia

D. Schizoaffective Disorder, Depressive Type

E. None of the above

2. Which of the following medications has FDA approval for use in this disorder once the patient turns 18?

A. Haldol

B. Risperidone

C. Quetiapine

D. Lurasidone

E. Paliperidone

3. What is the estimated lifetime prevalence of this disorder?

A. 0.1%

B. 0.2%

C. 0.3%

D. 0.4%

E. 0.5%

4. Which of the following tools is likely to be the most helpful in this case?

A. PANSS

B. SCARED

C. CARS

D. CY-BOCS

E. Vanderbilt

5. Which of the following statements about this disorder is accurate?

A. Incidence of this disorder in females and males is equal

B. Lifetime risk of suicide in this disorder is 10%

C. Incidence of this disorder is higher in females than males

D. Lifetime risk of suicide in this disorder is 2.5%

E. None of the above

6. Lurasidone should be taken with at least how many calories of food?

A. 150 calories

B. 200 calories

C. 250 calories

D. 300 calories

E. 350 calories

7. The patient's parent calls you stating that the patient is not responding well to the medication anymore. She reports that the only thing that has changed is that the patient started taking St. John's wort 3 weeks ago. Which CYP pathway is most likely being affected?

A. CYP1A2

B. CYP3A4

C. CYP2D6

D. CYP2C9

E. None of the above

References & Answers:

1. Answer D. The patient meets criteria for Schizoaffective Disorder, Depressive Type.

DSM-5. Schizophrenia Spectrum and Other Psychotic Disorders. Schizoaffective Disorder. Page 105 – 110

2. Answer E. Paliperidone is FDA approved for the treatment of Schizoaffective Disorder for patients age 18 and up.

Miller, Jacob N., Black, Donald. Schizoaffective Disorder: A Challenging Diagnosis. Current Psychiatry. Pages 30-37. Page 33.

3. Answer C. The estimated lifetime prevalence of this disorder is 0.3%.

DSM-5. Schizophrenia Spectrum and Other Psychotic Disorders. Schizoaffective Disorder. Page 105 – 110. Page 107.

4. Answer A. The PANSS (Positive and Negative Syndrome Scale).

McClellan, Jon. Psychosis in Children & Adolescents. J Am Acad Child Adolesc Psychiatry 2018;57(5):308–312.

5. Answer C. Incidence of this disorder is higher in females than males.

DSM-5. Schizophrenia Spectrum and Other Psychotic Disorders. Schizoaffective Disorder. Page 105 – 110. Page 107-109.

6. Answer E. It is recommended to eat at least 350 Calories of food.

Lurasidone (Latuda) Package Insert. 12-2019. https://www.latuda.com/LatudaPrescribingInformation.pdf. Date Accessed: 03-24-2021.

7. Answer B. St. John's Wort is a strong CYP3A4 inducer, taking it together with Lurasidone would likely decrease the effect of Lurasidone.

Lurasidone (Latuda) Package Insert. 12-2019. https://www.latuda.com/LatudaPrescribingInformation.pdf. Date Accessed: 03-24-2021.

Case 32

A 4 year old child brought in by his parents for evaluation of his behavior at daycare. His parents report that they get daily calls from the day care that he is too energetic and restless. He has a hard time being quiet during quiet time and reading time. He constantly interrupts and talks over other children and day care staff. He often climbs on the furniture. Whenever he is seated, he will tap his feet constantly. During games like duck-duck-goose or hide and go seek, he has a hard time being patient. At home his parents report that they notice similar things but they do their best to handle it. He does get frustrated when he is told to behave and calm down.

Multiple Choice Questions:

1. What is the diagnosis or diagnoses? – Choose all answers that apply

A. Disruptive Mood Dysregulation Disorder

B. Attention Deficit Hyperactivity Disorder

C. Intellectual Disability Disorder

D. Generalized Anxiety Disorder

E. None of the above

2. Which of the following treatment options would be appropriate?

A. Clonidine

B. Guanfacine

C. Atomoxetine

D. Dextroamphetamine

E. Lisdexamfetamine

3. The mother calls you a few months to tell you that she heard about an ADHD medication that can be used as patch, which of the following is she likely talking about?

A. Methylphenidate

B. Amphetamine

C. Dextroamphetamine

D. Guanfacine

E. None of the Above

4. Which ADHD presentation is more common in preschoolers?

A. Inattentive Presentation

B. Hyperactive Presentation

C. Combined Presentation

5. What ADHD presentation is more common in elementary age children?

A. Inattentive Presentation

B. Hyperactive Presentation

C. Combined Presentation

6. What ADHD presentation is more common in high school age children?

A. Inattentive Presentation

B. Hyperactive Presentation

C. Combined Presentation

References & Answers:

1. **Answer B.** This patient meets the criteria for ADHD.

DSM-5. Neurodevelopmental Disorders. ADHD. Page 59-65.

2. **Answer D.** Dextroamphetamine is an FDA approved medication for the treatment of ADHD for this patient's age. The other medications are not FDA approved for this age group. That being said some parents and clinicians may opt for trying CBT for ADHD or Parent Management Training prior to initiating medication in a patient this young.

Dexedrine. FDA Package Insert. 12-2019. https://www.accessdata.fda.gov/drugsatfda_docs/label/2019/017078s052lbl.pdf Date Accessed: 3/31/2021.

Lewis's Child & Adolescent Psychiatry Textbook. 5th Edition. 2018. Chapter 5.1. Page 374 - 382.

3. **Answer A.** There is a patch version of Methylphenidate that can be used in patients.

Lewis's Child & Adolescent Psychiatry Textbook. 5th Edition. 2018. Chapter 5.1. Page 376.

4. **Answer B.** The Hyperactive Presentation of ADHD is the most common presentation in Pre-Schoolers.

Lewis's Child & Adolescent Psychiatry Textbook. 5th Edition. 2018. Chapter 5.1. Page 365.

5. **Answer C.** The Combined Presentation of ADHD is the most common presentation in elementary age children.

Lewis's Child & Adolescent Psychiatry Textbook. 5th Edition. 2018. Chapter 5.1. Page 365.

6. **Answer A.** The Inattentive Presentation is the more common in high schoolers.

Lewis's Child & Adolescent Psychiatry Textbook. 5th Edition. 2018. Chapter 5.1. Page 365.

Case 33

A 17-year-old girl who presents with her mother to talk about the patient's feelings toward her mom. The parent reports that 10 days ago she found out that her daughter was dating a girl. The parent is okay with the patient dating a girl but did not like the fact that the patient was keeping it a secret from her. The patient reports that she feels sad and hurt that her mother read her private diary to find out who she was dating. She feels like her mother betrayed her trust and thinks her mother is being too nosy. Since this happened the patient has switched to a virtual journal that is locked with a password. The parent is concerned that now the patient seems irritated at her on most days and is unwilling to forgive her. The patient reports that she is considering moving out when she is 18, since she can no longer trust her mom to respect her privacy. She continues to do well in school and her after school job, and still enjoys hanging out with her friends.

Multiple Choice Questions:

1. What is the diagnosis or diagnoses? – Choose all answers that apply

A. Major Depressive Disorder

B. Disruptive Mood Dysregulation Disorder

C. Borderline Personality Disorder

D. Paranoid Personality Disorder

E. None of the Above

2. In a follow up visit 1 week later, the patient tells you that she identifies as LGBTQ+. Suicide attempts are believed to be how much more likely in youth who identify as LGBTQ+ versus patients who identify as heterosexual?

A. 2 times

B. 3 times

C. 4 times

D. 5 times

E. 6 times

3. 2 weeks later, the patient reports to you that she is not as mad at her mother anymore. However, she reports that her family does not seem to support her identification as LGBTQ+ and this frustrates her. She reports drinking one beer a day in order to decrease her frustration. Which of the following tools can be helpful in assessing substance use?

A. PHQ-9

B. GAD-7

C. CRAFFT

D. YMRS

E. CYBOCS

F. None of the Above

4. Which of the following laboratory orders can be helpful in assessing her alcohol use?

A. HbA1c

B. TSH

C. HDL

D. CDT

E. None of the Above

5. In order to meet criteria for Moderate Alcohol Use Disorder, how many symptoms are required per the DSM-5?

A. 2

B. 3

C. 4

D. 5

E. 6

References & Answers:

1. **Answer E.** Parent-Child Relational Problem (V61.20) (Z62.820). There is no diagnosable condition based on the history we have. It would not be unreasonable for the patient to be irritated at her mother for invading her privacy.

DSM-5. Other Conditions That May be a Focus of Clinical Attention. Problems Related to Family Upbringing. Pages 714.

2. **Answer C.** Suicide attempts are thought to be 4 times as likely in youth who identify as LGBTQ+.

LGBTQ+. Anxiety & Depression Association of America. https://adaa.org/find-help/by-demographics/lgbtq#Facts. Date Accessed: 03/30/2021

3. **Answer C.** The CRAFFT can be used to help assess substance use.

Dulcan, M.K. Dulcan's Textbook of Child and Adolescent Psychiatry. 2nd Edition 2016. Chapter 12. Evaluation Section.

4. **Answer D.** CDT (carbohydrate-deficient transferrin) is a lab order that can be used to help assess alcohol use. Elevated CDTs are associated with Chronic Alcohol Use.

Allen, J.P., et al. Biomarkers of Heavy Drinking. NIH. National Institute on Alcohol Abuse and Alcoholism. https://pubs.niaaa.nih.gov/publications/assessingalcohol/biomarkers.htm. Date Accessed: 03/30/2021.

5. **Answer C.** In order to meet the criteria for Moderate Alcohol Use Disorder, 4 symptoms are required.

DSM-5. Substance-Related Disorders. Alcohol-Related Disorders. Page 490 - 497.

Case 34

A 16-year-old male brought in by his family for self esteem problems. His parents report that the patient is hard on himself and does not like the way he looks. The patient reports that he got tired of people making fun of his weight, so he made it his goal to lose weight and eat better. He used to weigh 150 lbs and now weighs 100 lbs; the weight was lost over 6 months. He was able to the lose the weight by only eating one meal a day and exercising at least 2 hours a day. He reports that he looks better now and has even further room for improvement in his looks and weight. His parents want him to eat more than one meal a day which he refuses, since he is worried about gaining weight and looking unhealthy. He is 5 ft 5 inches.

Multiple Choice Questions:

1. What is the diagnosis or diagnoses? – Choose all answers that apply

A. Binge Eating Disorder

B. Bulimia Nervosa

C. Avoidant/Restrictive Food Intake Disorder

D. Rumination Disorder

E. None of the Above

2. Which of the following therapies would be most appropriate for this patient?

A. Dialectical Behavioral Therapy

B. Family Based Treatment

C. Psychodynamic Therapy

D. Interpersonal Therapy

E. None of the above

3. Which of the following medications is FDA approved to treat the patient's condition?

A. Sertraline

B. Fluoxetine

C. Olanzapine

D. Quetiapine

E. None of the above

4. Which of the following tools could be helpful in screening for this disorder?

A. PHQ-9

B. GAD-7

C. CYBOCS

D. EDE-Q

E. None of the Above

5. Which of the following findings would suggest that inpatient treatment is likely appropriate?

A. Weight <90 % of expected body weight

B. Weight <85 % of expected body weight

C. Weight <80 % of expected body weight

D. Weight <75 % of expected body weight

6. The patient is admitted to the hospital and unfortunately develops refeeding syndrome. Which of the following electrolytes is thought to play a key role in developing refeeding syndrome?

A. Sodium

B. Potassium

C. Chloride

D. Phosphorous

E. None of the above

References & Answers:

1. Answer E. The patient meets criteria for Anorexia Nervosa. Additionally, based on the height and weight provided, the BMI is 16.6, placing the BMI-for-age at the 2nd percentile for boys aged 16 years. This child is underweight.

DSM-5. Feeding and Eating Disorders. Anorexia Nervosa. Pages 338-339.

2. Answer B. Family Based Treatment is a therapy that has been found to be helpful in the treatment of eating disorders like Anorexia Nervosa.

Dulcan, M.K. Dulcan's Textbook of Child and Adolescent Psychiatry. 2nd Edition 2016. Chapter 20.

3. Answer E. There are no FDA approved medications for the treatment of Anorexia Nervosa.

Dulcan, M.K. Dulcan's Textbook of Child and Adolescent Psychiatry. 2nd Edition 2016. Chapter 20.

Lewis's Child & Adolescent Psychiatry Textbook. 5th Edition. 2018. Chapter 5.7.1. Page 548-562.

4. Answer D. The Eating Disorders Examination-Questionnaire (EDE-Q) can be helpful in screening for eating disorders.

Lock, J., et al. Practice Parameter for the Assessment and Treatment of Children and Adolescents With Eating Disorders. J. Am. Acad. Child Adolesc. Psychiatry, 2015;54(5):412–425.

5. Answer D. Weight <75 % of expected body weight is a finding that can indicate that inpatient treatment is likely.

Rome, Ellen S., Strandjord, Sarah E. Eating Disorders. Pediatrics in Review. 2016. Vol. 37. No. 8. 323 – 334.

6. Answer D. Phosphorus is thought to play a role in the development of refeeding syndrome. As Phosphorus levels are already low in patients who have experienced prolonged undernutrition, when refeeding happens Phosphorous is brought into cells to generate ATP, further depleting the levels of available Phosphorous.

Rome, Ellen S., Strandjord, Sarah E. Eating Disorders. Pediatrics in Review. 2016. Vol. 37. No. 8. 323 – 334.

Case 35

A 15 year old girl presents for evaluation with her parents regarding a concern about her behavior. The parents report that for the past 3 months the patient has been stress eating. They've noticed that she will eat portions of food that are enough for several people, usually once to twice a week at dinner time. The patient reports that she feels the urge to do this and is not able to control it. Her mother has noticed that after eating the big portions of food the patient will usually go to the bathroom, and she has heard her vomit. The patient reports that the vomiting helps her clear out the excess food and thinks her parents are making this a bigger deal than it is. She wants to make sure her body does not look overweight. They report no change in her weight over the past 3 months.

Multiple Choice Questions:

1. What is the diagnosis or diagnoses? – Choose all answers that apply

A. Binge Eating Disorder

B. Anorexia Nervosa

C. Avoidant/Restrictive Food Intake Disorder

D. Rumination Disorder

E. None of the Above

2. Which of the following medications is approved to treat the patient's disorder?

A. Sertraline

B. Fluoxetine

C. Venlafaxine

D. Fluvoxamine

E. None of the above

3. Which of the following therapies would be most appropriate for this patient?

A. Dialectical Behavioral Therapy

B. Psychoanalysis

C. Psychodynamic Therapy

D. Interpersonal Therapy

E. None of the above

4. In which of the following groups is the prevalence of this disorder the highest?

A. African American

B. Hispanic

C. Asian

D. Caucasian

E. None of the Above

5. You examine the patient's teeth and find evidence of dental damage from the patient's reported purging, what is the term for this?

A. Mallory Weiss Tear

B. Oral Mucositis

C. Cheilitis

D. Perimyolysis

E. None of the above

6. In patients with this disorder what is the estimated occurrence of Sialadenosis?

A. 10 % - 25 %

B. 25 % - 30 %

C. 35 % - 40 %

D. 45 % - 50 %

E. None of the above

7. In patients with this disorder who abuse laxatives what acid base state are they most likely to develop initially?

A. Hypochloremic Metabolic Acidosis

B. Hypochloremic Metabolic Alkalosis

C. Hyperchloremic Metabolic Acidosis

D. Hyperchloremic Metabolic Alkalosis

References & Answers:

1. **Answer E.** The patient meets the criteria for Bulimia Nervosa.

DSM-5. Feeding and Eating Disorders. Bulimia Nervosa. Pages 345-350.

2. **Answer E.** Unfortunately at this time there are no FDA approved medications to treat Bulimia Nervosa in Children. In adults Fluoxetine is FDA Approved to treat Bulimia Nervosa.

Gorrell, Sasha. Le Grange, Daniel. Updated on Treatments of Adolescent Bulimia Nervosa. Child Adolesc Psychiatric Clin N Am 28 (2019) 537–547

3. **Answer E.** Family Based Treatment is a therapy that has been found to be helpful in the treatment of eating disorders like Bulimia Nervosa.

Gorrell, Sasha. Le Grange, Daniel. Updated on Treatments of Adolescent Bulimia Nervosa. Child Adolesc Psychiatric Clin N Am 28 (2019) 537–547

4. **Answer B.** The prevalence of Bulimia Nervosa is highest in Hispanics.

Castillo, Marigol. Weiselberg, Eric. Bulimia Nervosa/Purging Disorder. Curr Probl Pediatr Adolesc HealthCare2017;47:85-94

5. **Answer D.** The term for this is Perimyolysis.

Castillo, Marigol. Weiselberg, Eric. Bulimia Nervosa/Purging Disorder. Curr Probl Pediatr Adolesc HealthCare2017;47:85-94

6. **Answer A.** The estimated occurrence of Sialadenosis is between 10 % - 25 %. Sialadenosis is swelling of the parotid glands.

Castillo, Marigol. Weiselberg, Eric. Bulimia Nervosa/Purging Disorder. Curr Probl Pediatr Adolesc HealthCare2017;47:85-94

7. **Answer C.** The acid base state they are most likely to develop initially is Hypercholremic Metabolic Acidosis.

Castillo, Marigol. Weiselberg, Eric. Bulimia Nervosa/Purging Disorder. Curr Probl Pediatr Adolesc HealthCare2017;47:85-94

Case 36

A 14-year-old boy who presents for evaluation of his eating habits. His parents report that he eats too much food in one sitting almost every day and eats too fast. This has been going on for 6 months. The patient reports that he feels like he cannot control the feeling to eat a lot. For the past few months, he eats some of his meals in secret to avoid being chastised and embarrassed by his parents. Sometimes he eats when he is not hungry and feels bad about it afterwards.

Multiple Choice Questions:

1. What is the diagnosis or diagnoses? – Choose all answers that apply

A. Bulimia Nervosa

B. Anorexia Nervosa

C. Avoidant/Restrictive Food Intake Disorder

D. Rumination Disorder

E. None of the Above

2. Which of the following medications is FDA approved to treat the patient's disorder?

A. Fluoxetine

B. Sertraline

C. Lisdexamfetamine

D. Methylphenidate

E. None of the above

3. Which of the following therapies would be most appropriate for this patient?

A. Psychodynamic Psychotherapy

B. Psychoanalysis

C. Supportive Psychotherapy

D. Cognitive Behavioral Therapy

E. None of the above

4. In this class of psychiatric disorders, the patient's disorder is:

A. Less prevalent in males than females

B. More prevalent in males than females

C. Equally prevalent in males and females

D. More prevalent in females than males

E. None of the above

References & Answers:

1. **Answer E.** The patient meets the criteria for Binge Eating Disorder.

DSM-5. Feeding and Eating Disorders. Binge Eating Disorder. Pages 350-353.

2. **Answer E.** There are no medications that are FDA approved for Binge Eating Disorder in Children & Adolescents

Lewis's Child & Adolescent Psychiatry Textbook. 5th Edition. 2018. Chapter 5.7.1. Page 548 - 562. 559.

3. **Answer D.** Cognitive Behavioral Therapy would be the most appropriate therapy for the patient.

Lewis's Child & Adolescent Psychiatry Textbook. 5th Edition. 2018. Chapter 5.7.1. Page 548 - 562. 559.

4. **Answer D.** The patient's disorder is more prevalent in females than in males.

Bohon, Cara. Binge Eating Disorder in Children and Adolescents. Child Adolesc Psychiatric Clin N Am 28 (2019) 549–555. Pg 553.

Case 37

A 7-year-old boy is brought in by his parents for odd behaviors. The parents report that for the past 6 months that after the whole family has gone to sleep the child gets up out of bed and walks around the house. They have noticed that he will usually have a blank look on his face, walks around the house for a few minutes, and then goes back to bed. He does not remember these episodes happening and does not respond to his parents when he is having these episodes. He has been a healthy child his whole life and is taking no medications. His parents wonder what is going on and are concerned that he might injure himself.

Multiple Choice Questions:

1. What is the diagnosis or diagnoses? – Choose all answers that apply

A. Nightmare Disorder

B. Non-Rapid Eye Movement Sleep Arousal Disorder

C. Rapid Eye Movement Sleep Behavior Disorder

D. Narcolepsy

E. None of the Above

2. What is the estimated prevalence of this disorder?

A. 1% - 2%

B. 1% - 3%

C. 1% - 4%

D. 1% - 5%

E. None of the above

3. What is the typical age range of onset of this disorder?

A. 2 – 4 years of age

B. 4 – 6 years of age

C. 6 – 8 years of age

D. None of the above

4. What is the peak time of occurrence of this disorder?

A. First 1/3 of night

B. First 1/2 of night

C. Last 1/3 of night

D. Last ½ of night

E. None of the above

5. What treatment option is the most appropriate to recommend at this time?

A. Reassurance and discuss Environmental Safety

B. Prescribe Clonazepam

C. Prescribe Paroxetine

D. Advise the parent to interrupt the episode and wake the patient up

E. None of the above

References & Answers:

1. **Answer B.** He meets the criteria for NREM Sleep Walking (Non-Rapid Eye Movement Sleep Arousal Disorder.

DSM-5. Sleep-Wake Disorders. Non-Rapid Eye Movement Sleep Arousal Disorders. Pages 399-404.

2. **Answer D.** 1% - 5% is the estimated prevalence of this disorder.

DSM-5. Sleep-Wake Disorders. Non-Rapid Eye Movement Sleep Arousal Disorders. Pages 399-404. Page 401.

3. **Answer D.** 4 – 12 years of age is the typical age range of onset of this disorder.

Nevsimalova, Sona., Bruni, Oliviero. Sleep Disorders in Children. Chapter 14. Parasomnias in Children. Page 313.

4. **Answer A.** The peak time of occurrence of this disorder is the first 1/3 of night.

Nevsimalova, Sona., Bruni, Oliviero. Sleep Disorders in Children. Chapter 14. Parasomnias in Children. Page 313.

5. **Answer A.** Reassurance and discuss Environmental Safety. Most children grow out of the disorder in adolescence.

Nevsimalova, Sona., Bruni, Oliviero. Sleep Disorders in Children. Chapter 14. Parasomnias in Children. Page 321-323.

Case 38

A 16 year old girl who has been having trouble with her sleep arrives for an evaluation. She reports that for the past 2 years she has had trouble going to sleep at the time she wants during the school year. She reports that she starts feeling sleepy at 3 AM, but she would like to be asleep by 10 PM. She reports falling asleep at 3 AM and having to wake up for school at 6 AM, this has made it difficult for her to get to school on time and her grades have declined. She tends to be very sleepy throughout the weekdays because of her sleep problems. She sometimes drinks coffee to help her get through her day at school. On the weekends her sleep is much better and not problematic because she can go to sleep at 3 AM and wake up later in the day and functions well on the weekends.

Multiple Choice Questions:

1. What is the diagnosis or diagnoses? – Choose all answers that apply

A. Insomnia Disorder

B. Non-Rapid Eye Movement Sleep Arousal Disorder

C. Rapid Eye Movement Sleep Behavior Disorder

D. Narcolepsy

E. None of the Above

2. In what way does Caffeine influence sleep?

A. Counter acts the function of Adenosine

B. Counter acts the function of Serotonin

C. Counter acts the function of Dopamine

D. Counter acts the function of Norepinephrine

E. None of the above

3. The parent and patient ask you how Melatonin influences sleep, which of the following is the most appropriate answer?

A. Melatonin is anti-hypnotic and should not be prescribed

B. Melatonin increases with increased light before bedtime

C. Melatonin has no influence on sleep

D. Melatonin is secreted by the Anterior Pituitary Gland and helps you fall asleep

E. None of the above

4. Which of the following Questionnaires would be most helpful in this case?

A. PHQ-9

B. GAD-7

C. CYBOCS

D. MCTQ

E. None of the above

5. The patient asks you if intense exercise before bed time might help them sleep better, which of the following is the most appropriate response?

A. Intense exercise before bed time will help them fall asleep

B. Intense exercise before bedtime has not effect on sleep

C. Intense exercise before bedtime will likely make it harder for them to sleep

D. Intense exercise before bedtime will likely make it easier for them to sleep

E. None of the above

References & Answers:

1. **Answer E.** She meets criteria for Circadian Rhythm Sleep Wake Disorder - Delayed Sleep Phase Type

DSM-5. Sleep-Wake Disorders. Circadian Rhythm Sleep-Wake Disorders. Pages 390-398.

2. **Answer A.** Counter acts the function of Adenosine at the Adenosine Receptor and helps promote wakefulness.

Feder, Michael A., Baroni, Argelinda. Identifying and Treating Delayed Sleep Phase Disorder in Adolescents. Child Adolesc Psychiatric Clin N Am 30 (2021) 159–174.

3. **Answer E.** Melatonin is suppressed by bright lights before bedtime. Melatonin does have hypnotic properties and can help adjust sleep phase to the desired time. Melatonin is secreted by the Pineal Gland.

Feder, Michael A., Baroni, Argelinda. Identifying and Treating Delayed Sleep Phase Disorder in Adolescents. Child Adolesc Psychiatric Clin N Am 30 (2021) 159–174.

4. **Answer D.** MCTQ (Munich Chrono-Type Questionnaire) would be the most helpful. It helps identify the patient's primary sleep times and helps identify which of the seven chronotypes they might be.

Feder, Michael A., Baroni, Argelinda. Identifying and Treating Delayed Sleep Phase Disorder in Adolescents. Child Adolesc Psychiatric Clin N Am 30 (2021) 159–174.

5. **Answer C.** Intense exercise before bedtime will likely make it harder for them to sleep, since intense exercise before bedtime can suppress Melatonin release.

Feder, Michael A., Baroni, Argelinda. Identifying and Treating Delayed Sleep Phase Disorder in Adolescents. Child Adolesc Psychiatric Clin N Am 30 (2021) 159–174.

Case 39

A 7 year old girl brought in by her parents because of problems with sleepiness. They report that for the past 6 months teachers have been calling them several times a week to tell them that the patient is falling asleep in class. The patient reports that most days she has times where she feels very sleepy and must sleep, despite having had a good night's sleep. Her classmates have also started making fun of her because at times when she laughs, she will lose control of her body and fall to the floor and is not able to get up for about a minute.

Multiple Choice Questions:

1. What is the likely diagnosis or diagnoses? – Choose all answers that apply

A. Insomnia Disorder

B. Non-Rapid Eye Movement Sleep Arousal Disorder

C. Rapid Eye Movement Sleep Behavior Disorder

D. Narcolepsy

E. None of the Above

2. Which of the following HLAs are a risk factor for Narcolepsy?

A. HLA DQB1*06:02

B. HLA DQB1*05:01

C. HLA-B*1502

D. HLA-A*2402

E. None of the above

3. Which of the following is believed to the be the peak of onsets of these disorders?

A. 10 – 15 & 15 – 20 years of age

B. 15 – 25 & 30 – 35 years of age

C. 5 – 10 & 10 – 15 years of age

D. 15 – 20 & 25 – 30 years of age

E. None of the above

4. Which of the following medications would be most appropriate in this case?

A. Methylphenidate

B. Armodafinil

C. Sodium Oxybate

D. Modafinil

E. None of the above

5. Which of the following would be most appropriate to help you confirm the diagnosis?

A. CT

B. MRI

C. MSLT

D. PET Scan

E. SPECT Scan

6. This disorder can be attributed to problems in which Brain System?

A. Dopaminergic

B. Noradrenergic

C. Gabaergic

D. Orexinergic

E. None of the above

References & Answers:

1. **Answer D.** She meets the criteria for Narcolepsy.

DSM-5. Sleep-Wake Disorders. Narcolepsy. Pages 372-378.

2. **Answer A.** HLA DQB1*06:02 is a risk factor for Narcolepsy.

Nevsimalova, Sona., Bruni, Oliviero. Sleep Disorders in Children. Chapter 3. Epidemiology of sleep disorders in children and adolescents. Page 56.

3. **Answer B.** Peak ages of onset are believed to be between 15 – 25 & 30 – 35 years of age

DSM-5. Sleep-Wake Disorders. Narcolepsy. Pages 372-378. Page 375.

4. **Answer A.** Methylphenidate would be the most appropriate medication for this age group. It has FDA approval for Narcolepsy in children. Atomoxetine also has FDA approval for treatment of Narcolepsy in children.

Nevsimalova, Sona., Bruni, Oliviero. Sleep Disorders in Children. Chapter 13. Disorders Associated with Increased Sleepiness. Page 290-291.

5. **Answer C.** MSLT (Multiple Sleep Latency Test) – helps identify excessive daytime sleepiness by measuring how quickly you fall asleep.

Nevsimalova, Sona., Bruni, Oliviero. Sleep Disorders in Children. Chapter 13. Disorders Associated with Increased Sleepiness. Page 290-291. Page 287.

Answer:

6. **Answer D.** Problems in the Orexinergic system in the Brain has been attributed to Narcolepsy.

Trosman, Irina., Ivanenko, Anna. Classification and Epidemiology of sleep disorders in children and adolescents Child Adolesc Psychiatric Clin N Am 30 (2021) 47–64. Page 49.

Case 40

A 6-year-old girl brought in by her parents for help with her behavior. Her parents report that the patient does not seem to be careful around adults she does not know. She will often sit on the laps of adults that are not her family members despite her parents telling her not to do that. She also approaches adults she does not know and interacts with them like if she has known them her whole life. They think she would likely go off with strangers willingly if they did not keep an eye on her. The child was adopted at age 4, her biological parents would often leave her alone and would neglect to feed her.

Multiple Choice Questions:

1. What is the diagnosis or diagnoses? – Choose all answers that apply

A. Oppositional Defiant Disorder

B. Conduct Disorder

C. Reactive Attachment Disorder

D. Disruptive Mood Dysregulation Disorder

E. None of the above

2. At what developmental age is the earliest you can diagnose this disorder?

A. 3 months

B. 6 months

C. 9 months

D. 12 months

E. 15 months

3. At what developmental age is Stranger Anxiety thought to develop?

A. 4 months

B. 5 months

C. 6 months

D. 7 months

E. 8 months

4. Which of the following medications is approved for use in this disorder?

A. Fluoxetine

B. Paroxetine

C. Sertraline

D. Escitalopram

E. None of the Above

References & Answers:

1. **Answer E.** The patient meets criteria for Disinhibited Social Engagement Disorder

DSM-5. Trauma and Stressor Related Disorders. Disinhibited Social Engagement Disorder. Pages 268 - 269.

2. **Answer C.** Age 9 months is the earliest you can diagnose this disorder.

DSM-5. Trauma and Stressor Related Disorders. Disinhibited Social Engagement Disorder. Pages 268 - 269. Page 269.

3. **Answer E.** Stranger anxiety is believed to develop around age 8 months.

Lewis's Child & Adolescent Psychiatry Textbook. 5th Edition. 2018. Chapter 2.1.1. The Infant and Toddler. Page 69-78.

4. **Answer E.** No medications are approved to treat Disinhibited Social Engagement Disorder.

Zeanah, C.H., et al. Practice Parameter for the Assessment and Treatment of Children and Adolescents With Reactive Attachment Disorder and Disinhibited Social Engagement Disorder. J Am Acad Child Adolesc Psychiatry 2016;55(11):990–1003.

Case 41

A 10-year-old boy brought in by his parents for him refusing to take off his hat. The patient's parents report that for the past 6 months he has been wearing a hat and refusing to take it off, except to shower. At first, they did not think it was problematic but one day they noticed that there was a bald patch on his head. The patient reports that he has been pulling his hair and has been using the hat to cover up the bald patch, since he did not want to get teased at school or worry his parents. He does not know why he pulls his hair but reports that he can not stop doing it, no matter how hard he tries not to.

Multiple Choice Questions:

1. What is the diagnosis or diagnoses? – Choose all answers that apply

A. Obsessive Compulsive Disorder

B. Excoriation Disorder

C. Trichotillomania

D. Body Dysmorphic Disorder

E. None of the above

2. Which of the following medications is approved for use in this disorder?

A. Fluoxetine

B. Venlafaxine

C. Clomipramine

D. Fluvoxamine

E. None of the above

3. Which of the following therapies would be most appropriate?

A. Dialectical Behavioral Therapy

B. Psychodynamic Psychotherapy

C. Mindfulness

D. Interpersonal Psychotherapy

E. None of the above

4. A few months later the patient and his parents report to you that the patient has developed abdominal pain and continues to pull his hair out. Additionally, the parents have seen him put hair into his mouth. What is the likely cause of the patient's abdominal pain?

A. Cholelithiasis

B. Kidney Stone

C. Trichobezoar

D. Gout

E. None of the above

References & Answers:

1. **Answer C.** He meets the criteria for Trichotillomania.

DSM-5. Obsessive Compulsive and Related Disorders. Trichotillomania. Pages 251-254.

2. **Answer E.** There are no approved medications to treat this disorder. However, there have been some studies that show some improvement in symptoms with medication treatment.

Lewis's Child & Adolescent Psychiatry Textbook. 5th Edition. 2018. Chapter 5.5.3. Page 531-534.

3. **Answer E.** Cognitive Behavioral Therapy or Habit Reversal Training would be the most appropriate choices for this patient.

Lewis's Child & Adolescent Psychiatry Textbook. 5th Edition. 2018. Chapter 5.5.3. Page 531-534.

4. **Answer C.** Trichobezoar is the likely cause of the patient's abdominal pain. The patient likely ingested a large amount of hair that caused the formation of the Trichobezoar.

Wang, Z., et al. The Diagnosis and Treatment of Rapunzel Syndrome. Acta Radiologica Open. 2016 Nov. 5(11) 1–4

Case 42

A 15-year-old girl is brought in by her parents for concerns about her behavior. They report that she was first diagnosed with Major Depressive Disorder about 2 years ago. She was treated with an antidepressant and her depression resolved within 12 months. She has been off the medication for about 6 months now. Their concern today is that there are times when her mood appears to be an out of the ordinary happiness and she is much more active. The patient reports that during these times she feels extremely good about herself, nothing can bring her down, and does not feel the need to sleep. Her parents also mention that during these times she talks too much, and it is hard to follow her thought process. The longest these concerning behaviors have lasted are about four to five days, and the last time this occurred was one month ago. She has been suspended from school several times in the past few months during the episodes for talking too much in class and attempting to take over classroom lessons from the teachers.

Multiple Choice Questions:

1. What is the diagnosis or diagnoses? – Choose all answers that apply

A. Disruptive Mood Dysregulation Disorder

B. Schizoaffective Disorder

C. Major Depressive Disorder

D. Bipolar I Disorder

E. None of the above

2. After providing the patient and parent with the diagnosis and treatment plan, they decided to decline treatment. One month later they return and report that she was hospitalized after becoming depressed and writing a suicide note. She was discharged on Lurasidone 20 mg daily which she has responded well to. In order to ensure optimal absorption of Lurasidone, which of the following statements is true?

A. Lurasidone must be taken at night on an empty stomach

B. Lurasidone must be taken in the morning on an empty stomach

C. Lurasidone should be taken with at least a 500-calorie meal

D. Lurasidone should be taken with at least a 300-calorie meal

E. None of the Above

3. The patient reports that when she first started the Lurasidone she felt her neck get very stiff, the doctor at the hospital gave her an intramuscular medication to help with the stiffness and she felt better within an hour. Which of the following is likely the medication she received?

A. Hydroxyzine

B. Haloperidol

C. Thorazine

D. Deutetrabenazine

E. None of the above

4. The patient returns in 3 months; she is pregnant and is continuing to take Lurasidone 20 mg daily. She asks if she can breast feed while taking Lurasidone, what is the most appropriate response to her question?

A. She should not breast feed while taking Lurasidone

B. Breast feeding while taking Lurasidone is completely safe

C. In order to breast feed her baby she should switch to another medication

D. There is some evidence that medications like Lurasidone are found at low levels in breast milk and her baby will require close monitoring if she decides to breast feed.

E. None of the above

References & Answers:

1. **Answer E.** She meets the criteria for Bipolar II Disorder

DSM-5. Bipolar and Related Disorders. Bipolar II Disorder. Pages 132-139.

2. **Answer E.** Lurasidone should be taken with at least 350 calories of food.

Lurasidone. FDA Package Insert. 12-2019.
https://www.accessdata.fda.gov/drugsatfda_docs/label/2019/200603s035lbl.pdf

Date Accessed: 4-24-2021.

3. **Answer E.** The most likely medication that was given to the patient for the acute dystonia she experienced is Benztropine. Another medication that might have been used is Diphenhydramine.

Lewis's Child & Adolescent Psychiatry Textbook. 5th Edition. 2018. Chapter 6.1.4.3. Page 732 – 741.

4. **Answer D.** Psychotropic medications are present in breast milk at varying levels. It is currently thought that antipsychotic use during pregnancy is relatively safe. Based on current research, levels of antipsychotics in breast milk are thought to be generally low. There is a lack of outcomes data on the usage of antipsychotics during breastfeeding and potential side effects. If the mother decides to breast feed while taking an antipsychotic, her baby will need to monitored closely.

Payne, Jennifer L. Psychopharmacology in Pregnancy and Breastfeeding. Med Clin N Am 103 (2019) 629–650. Pages: 629 – 650.

Case 43

A 6-year-old girl brought in by her parents for strange eating habits. The parents report that they have seen the patient eating candy wrappers and paper. For the past few months they have been watching her closely to make sure she does not eat these things but she always manages to find a way to eat them, they have found bits of paper and candy wrappers hidden in her room. They have asked her why she does this and she has said that she does not know. Her teacher at school has also called the parents to tell them that they have seen her eat paper at school.

Multiple Choice Questions:

1. What is the diagnosis or diagnoses? – Choose all answers that apply

A. Intellectual Disability

B. Autism Spectrum Disorder

C. Disruptive Mood Dysregulation Disorder

D. Encopresis

E. None of the above

2. Which of the following would be most appropriate to use in this case?

A. PHQ-9

B. GAD-7

C. PARDI

D. SCARED

E. None of the above

3. Which of the following therapies would be most appropriate in this case?

A. Dialectical Behavioral Therapy

B. Applied Behavioral Analysis

C. Psychodynamic Psychotherapy

D. Interpersonal Psychotherapy

E. None of the above

4. Which of the following has a known association with Pica?

A. Glucose Levels

B. Iron Levels

C. TSH Levels

D. Prolactin Levels

E. None of the above

References & Answers:

1. **Answer E.** She meets the criteria for Pica.

DSM-5. Feeding and Eating Disorders. Pica. Pages 329-331.

2. **Answer C.** PARDI – Pica, ARFID, and Rumination Disorder Interview, can be used to diagnose and assess the severity of these disorders in patients age 2 and up.

Lewis's Child & Adolescent Psychiatry Textbook. 5th Edition. 2018. Chapter 5.7.2. Page 562 - 568.

3. **Answer B.** The most appropriated therapy for this case would be ABA – Applied Behavioral Analysis.

Lewis's Child & Adolescent Psychiatry Textbook. 5th Edition. 2018. Chapter 5.7.2. Page 562 - 568.

4. **Answer B.** Iron levels – Iron Deficiency Anemia is associated with Pica. Ordering a CBC and Iron Levels would be helpful in this case.

Lewis's Child & Adolescent Psychiatry Textbook. 5th Edition. 2018. Chapter 5.7.2. Page 562 - 568.

Case 44

A 6 year old child brought in by her parents for problems at home and school. The parents report that patient often wets the bed at night, at least 3 times a week and has also been wetting herself at school at least once a week. This has been going on for almost a year now. When asked why this happens the patient states that sometimes she just wakes up wet. While at school sometimes she can not help it.

Multiple Choice Questions:

1. What is the diagnosis or diagnoses? – Choose all answers that apply

A. Encopresis

B. Enuresis

C. Oppositional Defiant Disorder

D. Conduct Disorder

E. None of the above

2. After age 5 what is the estimated rate of spontaneous remission of this disorder?

A. 1 % – 5 %

B. 5 % – 10 %

C. 10 % - 15 %

D. 1% - 2 %

E. None of the above

3. Previous treatment records suggest that the patient is healthy and has no underlying medication condition that could be contributing to her symptoms. Which of the following is a recommended treatment option?

A. Bell and Pad Method

B. Parent Child Interactive Therapy

C. Group Therapy

D. Cognitive Behavioral Therapy

E. None of the Above

4. After months of the treatment, picked in question 3, the patient continues to have trouble with wetting the bed at night and wetting herself in class. Which of the following medications is the most appropriate treatment recommendation?

A. Clomipramine

B. Prazosin

C. Finasteride

D. Amitriptyline

E. None of the above

References & Answers:

1. **Answer B.** The patient meets criteria for Enuresis.

DSM-5. Elimination Disorders. Enuresis. Page 355 -357

2. **Answer B**. After age 5 the spontaneous rate of remission for this disorder is 5% - 10 %

DSM-5. Elimination Disorders. Enuresis. Page 355 -357

3. **Answer A.** The Bell and Pad Method is a reasonable first step approach. If this does not help medication management can be considered.

Lewis's Child & Adolescent Psychiatry Textbook. 5th Edition. 2018. Chapter 5.12. Page 612 – 624.

4. **Answer E.** Imipramine and DDAVP would be reasonable choices. Before starting Imipramine, you should order an EKG. There is a risk of hyponatremia with DDAVP.

Lewis's Child & Adolescent Psychiatry Textbook. 5th Edition. 2018. Chapter 5.12. Page 612 – 624.

Case 45

A 5-year-old boy brought in by his parents for behavioral problems. His parents report that he has been defecating around the house for at least 6 months now. They will sometimes find feces in his underwear and in random areas around the house. The patient states that he can not control it and says he feels embarrassed by this. His Pediatrician examined him and could not find a reason why he was doing this. Overall they report he is healthy child and takes no medications.

Multiple Choice Questions:

1. What is the diagnosis or diagnoses? – Choose all answers that apply

A. Enuresis

B. Oppositional Defiant Disorder

C. Intellectual Disability

D. Encopresis

E. None of the above

2. What is the estimated prevalence of this disorder in 5 year olds?

A. 1%

B. 2%

C. 3%

D. 4%

E. 5%

3. Which of the following recommendations is the most appropriate in this case at this time?

A. Start Imipramine

B. Parent should punish the child

C. Provide the family with psychoeducation about the disorder and a behavioral treatment approach.

D. Parent should ignore the behavior

E. None of the above

References & Answers:

1. **Answer D.** The patient meets criteria for Encopresis.

DSM-5. Elimination Disorders. Encopresis. Page 357 – 359.

2. **Answer A.** The estimated prevalence of this disorder in 5 year olds is 1%.

DSM-5. Elimination Disorders. Encopresis. Page 357 – 359.

3. **Answer C.** Provide the family with psychoeducation about the disorder and a behavioral treatment approach.

Lewis's Child & Adolescent Psychiatry Textbook. 5th Edition. 2018. Chapter 5.12. Page 612 - 624.

Case 46

A 11-year-old girl brought in by her mother for behavioral problems that have been present for at least a year. The parent reports that the patient is often very argumentative with her and other adults. She has been suspended from school 6 times this academic year for arguing with her teachers and not following classroom rules. Whenever she makes a mistake or someone points out a mistake she has made, she is quick to blame others for the mistake. She gets easily annoyed when talking with adults. The patient reports that she does not like being told what to do and that she is usually in a good mood unless someone tries to boss her around.

1. What is the diagnosis or diagnoses? – Choose all answers that apply

A. Disruptive Mood Dysregulation Disorder

B. Bipolar Disorder

C. Conduct Disorder

D. Major Depressive Disorder

E. None of the above

2. Which of the following treatments would be most appropriate?

A. Psychodynamic Psychotherapy

B. Psychoanalysis

C. Parent Management Training

D. Dialectical Behavioral Therapy

E. Interpersonal Psychotherapy

3. Which of the following medications is approved for use in this disorder?

A. Fluoxetine

B. Risperidone

C. Sertraline

D. Quetiapine

E. None of the above

4. Which of the following disorders is thought to be the most comorbid with the disorder the patient has?

A. Intermittent Explosive Disorder

B. Bipolar Disorder

C. Attention Deficit Hyperactivity Disorder

D. Generalized Anxiety Disorder

E. None of the above

References & Answers:

1. **Answer E.** The patient meets the criteria for Oppositional Defiant Disorder.

DSM-5. Disruptive, Impulse-Control, and Conduct Disorders. Oppositional Defiant Disorder. Page 462 - 466.

2. **Answer C.** Parent Management Training. This type of treatment can be helpful in behavioral disorders such as Opposition Defiant Disorder, by trying to decrease problematic behaviors and promote prosocial behaviors. Another therapy that can be helpful is Multisystemic Therapy.

Lewis's Child & Adolescent Psychiatry Textbook. 5th Edition. 2018. Chapter 5.1.2. Page 387 – 398.

3. **Answer E.** There are no medications approved to treat Oppositional Defiant Disorder.

Lewis's Child & Adolescent Psychiatry Textbook. 5th Edition. 2018. Chapter 5.1.2. Page 387 – 398.

4. **Answer C.** Attention Deficit Hyperactive Disorder is thought to be the most co-morbid disorder with Oppositional Defiant Disorder.

Lewis's Child & Adolescent Psychiatry Textbook. 5th Edition. 2018. Chapter 5.1.2. Page 387 – 398.

Case 47

A 16-year-old boy is brought in by his parents after he got suspended from school. The parents report that the patient is out of control. He got suspended from school after his 5th fight with classmates. He beat up a classmate after getting into an argument with them. The parents report that teachers and other students have described him as a bully. The patient reports that he gets into fights at school when classmates will not comply with what he wants. The reason he was suspended this time for the fight in school was because he took his classmate's wallet. His parents grounded him for a month last summer for not coming home for 2 weeks. He refuses to say where he was or what he was doing during this time. His parents report that he has done this several times over the past 2 years. The parents report that they are baffled by his behavior, since he had no behavioral problems prior to starting high school.

Multiple Choice Questions:

1. What is the diagnosis or diagnoses? – Choose all answers that apply

A. Bipolar Disorder

B. Oppositional Defiant Disorder

C. Antisocial Personality Disorder

D. Conduct Disorder

E. None of the Above

2. Onset of this disorder is rare after which age?

A. 10

B. 12

C. 14

D. 16

E. None of the above

3. Which of the following predicts a worse outcome?

A. Co-morbidity with Major Depressive Disorder

B. Co-morbidity with Attention Deficit Hyperactivity Disorder

C. Co-morbidity with Generalized Anxiety Disorder

D. Co-morbidity with Adjustment Disorder

E. None of the above

4. Which of the following therapies is most likely to be helpful in this case?

A. Multisystemic Therapy

B. Dialectical Behavioral Therapy

C. Psychodynamic Psychotherapy

D. Interpersonal Therapy

E. None of the above

References & Answers:

1. **Answer D.** The patient meets criteria for Conduct Disorder

DSM-5. Disruptive, Impulse-Control, and Conduct Disorders. Oppositional Defiant Disorders. Page 469 - 475.

2. **Answer D.** Conduct Disorder onset is thought to be rare after age 16.

DSM-5. Disruptive, Impulse-Control, and Conduct Disorders. Oppositional Defiant Disorders. Page 469 - 475.

3. **Answer B.** Co-morbidity with Attention Deficit Hyperactivity Disorder is thought to predict a worse outcome in patient's with Conduct Disorder. Co-morbidity with Oppositional Defiant Disorder also is thought to predict a worse outcome in patient's with Conduct Disorder.

DSM-5. Disruptive, Impulse-Control, and Conduct Disorders. Oppositional Defiant Disorders. Page 469 - 475.

4. **Answer A.** Multisystemic Therapy can be helpful in patient's with Conduct Disorder, and has been found to decrease rates of drug use, out of home placement, and long term rate of criminal offenses.

Lewis's Child & Adolescent Psychiatry Textbook. 5th Edition. 2018. Chapter 5.1.2. Page 387 – 398.

Lewis's Child & Adolescent Psychiatry Textbook. 5th Edition. 2018. Chapter 6.2.7. Page 833 – 844.

Case 48

An 8-year-old girl is brought in by her parents for evaluation of learning problems. They report that she is behind in reading. Her teachers report that her reading, writing, and mathematics levels are at a 1st grade level, she is currently in 3rd grade. A psychologist did several tests at her school and reported to them that they believed the patient had a cognitive problem, but they were not sure what the psychologist meant by that. They report that she does not have friends at school and that her classmates often tease her and ask her to do things that get her in trouble – throw water on the floor or throw erasers at the teacher. She does not seem to understand that they are not being nice. In 1st and 2nd grade she did not seem to have problems with making friends or keeping up with the other children. There have been times were other children have tricked her into giving up her lunch money in exchange for paper clips.

Multiple Choice Questions:

1. What is the diagnosis or diagnoses? – Choose all answers that apply

A. Attention Deficit Hyperactivity Disorder

B. Social Communication Disorder

C. Intellectual Disability

D. Developmental Coordination Disorder

E. None of the Above

2. What is the estimated prevalence of this disorder?

A. 1%

B. 2%

C. 3%

D. 4%

E. None of the above

3. Which of the following is the most common genetic cause of the patient's disorder?

A. Fragile X Syndrome

B. Prader-Willi Syndrome

C. Velocardiofacial Syndrome

D. Trisomy 21

E. None of the Above

4. Which of the following would be helpful to measure adaptive functioning in this patient?

A. VABS

B. CARS

C. M-CHAT

D. CBCL

E. None of the Above

5. Which of the following medications is approved to treat this disorder?

A. Methylphenidate

B. Risperidone

C. Valproic Acid

D. Fluoxetine

E. None of the above

References & Answers:

1. **Answer C.** The most likely diagnosis the patient has is Intellectual Disability. She is performing at a 1ˢᵗ grade level despite being in 3ʳᵈ grade, previous psychological testing suggests cognitive problems, and is not able to understand when other children are not treating her appropriately.

DSM-5. Neurodevelopmental Disorders. Intellectual Disability. Page 33-41.

2. **Answer A.** The estimated prevalence of this disorder in the General Population is 1%.

DSM-5. Neurodevelopmental Disorders. Intellectual Disability. Page 33-41.

3. **Answer D.** Trisomy 21 (Down Syndrome) is the most common genetic cause of Intellectual Disability.

Lewis's Child & Adolescent Psychiatry Textbook. 5th Edition. 2018. Chapter 5.2.2. Page 433-443.

4. **Answer A.** The Vineland Adaptive Behavior Scales (VABS) would be a helpful scale to measure the patient's adaptive functioning.

Lewis's Child & Adolescent Psychiatry Textbook. 5th Edition. 2018. Chapter 5.2.2. Page 433-443.

5. **Answer E.** There are no medications approved to treat Intellectual Disability, however if the patient does meet criteria for other psychiatric disorders you should treat the co-morbid disorder with the appropriate medication.

Lewis's Child & Adolescent Psychiatry Textbook. 5th Edition. 2018. Chapter 5.2.2. Page 433-443.

Case 49

A 12-year-old girl is brought in by her parents for problems with her behavior. The parents report that two weeks ago they narrowly escaped a tornado while in the family car. Ever since then the patient has been having nightmares, but she has a hard time explaining what the nightmares are about. She is having a hard time concentrating at school and her grades have decreased. She reports that she feels very uncomfortable and nervous when the weather is brought up or the tornado. Staying asleep has become difficult for her. She can not remember how the family escaped the tornado, changes the channel whenever the weather is discussed, and has been refusing to get into the family car. She is very easily startled at school and seems to be always looking for the closest exit wherever she goes. She mentioned to her parents that she feels like something about herself has changed, she feels dazed.

Multiple Choice Questions:

1. What is the diagnosis or diagnoses? – Choose all answers that apply

A. Schizophrenia

B. Mild Neurocognitive Disorder

C. Post-Traumatic Stress Disorder

D. Dissociative Amnesia

E. None of the above

2. Which of the following is accurate about this disorder?

A. Prevalence of this disorder is greater in males than females.

B. Prevalence of this disorder is greater in females than males.

C. Prevalence of this disorder equal in males and females.

D. Prevalence of this disorder has not been studied.

E. None of the above.

3. Which of the following medication is approved to be used in this disorder?

A. Sertraline

B. Venlafaxine

C. Quetiapine

D. Fluoxetine

E. None of the above

References & Answers:

1. **Answer E.** None of the Above. The patient meets the criteria for Acute Stress Disorder. She experienced a traumatic event 2 weeks ago and has at least 9/14 Criteria B symptoms of Acute Distress Disorder.

 DSM-5. Trauma-and Stressor-Related Disorder. Acute Stress Disorder. Pages 280-286.

2. **Answer B.** Prevalence of this disorder is thought to be greater in females than males.

DSM-5. Trauma-and Stressor-Related Disorder. Acute Stress Disorder. Pages 280-286.

3. **Answer E.** None of the above. Currently there are no FDA approved medications to treat trauma disorders in children and adolescents. Therapies that can be helpful are Trauma Focused Therapies.

Lewis's Child & Adolescent Psychiatry Textbook. 5th Edition. 2018. Chapter 5.15.2. Pages 651-658.

Case 50

You are consulted about a 15-year-old boy currently in the hospital, the consulting team is concerned about his behavior. The patient's parents report that 2 weeks ago the patient reported not being able to move his right leg. The patient reports that one day he was just unable to move his right leg. The consulting team's extensive work up has been negative so far. On physical exam, the consulting team noted the presence of Hoover's sign. Overall, the parents report that the patient is a healthy, happy person. They do report that the patient has been very stressed this past month about taking standardized tests and his school finals coming up.

Multiple Choice Questions:

1. What is the diagnosis or diagnoses? – Choose all answers that apply

A. Factitious Disorder

B. Somatic Symptom Disorder

C. Illness Anxiety Disorder

D. Conversion Disorder

E. None of the Above

2. Which of the following about this disorder is true?

A. It is equally common in females and males

B. It is approximately 3-4 times more common in males than females

C. It is approximately 4-5 times more common in males than females

D. It is approximately 1-2 times more common in males than females

E. None of the above

3. The patient and family ask you if the patient will ever get better and what treatments are available, which of the following would be the most appropriate response?

A. The patient is pretending, and he will get better by tomorrow.

B. The patient will never get better.

C. The patient can be cured once he has electroconvulsive shock therapy.

D. The patient will get better once he starts taking an antidepressant.

E. None of the above

References & Answers:

1. **Answer D**. The most likely diagnosis is Conversion Disorder. His hospital workup and physical exam findings help support the diagnosis of Conversion Disorder. With the available information there is no indication that the patient is falsifying his symptoms, so Factious Disorder is less likely.

DSM-5. Somatic Symptom and Related Disorder. Conversion Disorder (Functional Neurological Symptom Disorder). Pages 318 - 321.

American Psychiatric Association. Conversion disorder (functional neurological symptom disorder). Diagnostic and Statistical Manual of Mental Disorders: DSM-5. 5th ed. Arlington, VA: American Psychiatric Publishing; 2013:318-321.

2. **Answer E.** None of the above. It is approximately 2-3 times more common in females than males.

DSM-5. Somatic Symptom and Related Disorder. Conversion Disorder (Functional Neurological Symptom Disorder). Pages 318 - 321.

3. **Answer E.** None of the above. The most appropriate response would be to explain to the patient and parent that Conversion Disorder is a term used to explain findings in patients were the physical symptoms they are experiencing are connected to complex interactions between the mind and body. It is also important to explain that the symptoms the patient is experiencing are real and that they are not making it up. One guideline suggests providing the patient and parent examples of biological reactions to stress: sweaty palms, shaky legs, and flushed cheeks, and explaining that in the case of Conversion Disorder, the patient is not consciously aware of the trigger/stressful event that is causing their symptoms. Regarding treatment, recommending the patient get back to their regular routines and in some cases, cognitive behavioral therapy can be helpful.

Lewis's Child & Adolescent Psychiatry Textbook. 5th Edition. 2018. Chapter 5.10. Page 591 – 604.

Krasnik, Catherine E., Meaney, Brandon., Grant, Christina. A clinical approach to paediatric conversion disorder: VEER in the right direction. Canadian Paediatric Surveillance Program. January 2013. https://www.cpsp.cps.ca/uploads/publications/RA-conversion-disorder.pdf Date Accessed: 04-24-2021.

Made in the USA
Coppell, TX
26 June 2024

33982716R00085